ASTD Trainer's WorkShop Series

Listening Skills
TRAINING

D0521022

Lisa J. Downs

ASTD
WORKPLACE LEARNING & PERFORMANCE
PRESS

ASTD Press is an internationally renowned source of insightful and practical information on workplace learning and performance topics, including training basics, evaluation and return on investment, instructional systems development, e-learning, leadership, and career development.

Ordering information: Books published by ASTD Press can be purchased by visiting our Website at store.astd.org or by calling 800.628.2783 or 703.683.8100.

Library of Congress Control Number: 2007931353

ISBN-10: 1-56286-502-1
ISBN-13: 978-1-56286-502-3

ASTD Press Editorial Staff:
Director: Cat Russo
Manager, Acquisitions and Author Relations: Mark Morrow
Editorial Manager: Jacqueline Edlund-Braun
Editorial Assistant: Maureen Soyars
Retail Trade Manager: Yelba Quinn
Developmental Editor: Carol Field
Indexer: Ken Hassman
Copyeditor and Proofreader: Ellen Newman
Interior Design and Production: Aptara, Inc.
Cover Design: Alizah Epstein
Cover Illustration: Patricia Languedoc

Printed by Victor Graphics, Inc., Baltimore, Maryland, www.victorgraphics.com

The ASTD Trainer's WorkShop Series is designed to be a practical, hands-on road map to help you quickly develop training in key business areas. Each book in the series offers all the exercises, handouts, assessments, structured experiences, and ready-to-use presentations needed to develop effective training sessions. In addition to easy-to-use icons, each book in the series includes a companion CD-ROM with PowerPoint presentations and electronic copies of all supporting material featured in the book.

C o n t e n t s

◆
_____

Chapter 12 STRUCTURED EXPERIENCES 145

Appendix USING THE COMPACT DISC 177

◆

When I began the process of researching for and writing this book, I remember wondering how I could possibly come up with enough information and activities focused solely on the topic of listening. Once I started to think about it, however, I realized that because there are so many aspects to listening, such as a having a clear process and using varied techniques, I wouldn't have any problem filling these pages. Listening is often a forgotten skill (or is at least one that we all assume we already have). It's one of the most important skills to learn and practice for effective communication, yet how often are we taught in school or in training programs how to really listen and given an opportunity to improve our listening ability? Not very often from what I remember about my own education. My guess is that many of you are in the same situation. Given this, I am delighted to provide you with what I hope is a useful resource to help you teach others how to improve their listening skills and to communicate more effectively. How well we listen has a great impact on how we resolve conflict, lead teams, and build relationships.

This book is organized in a way that allows trainers to easily focus their efforts on the needs of their learners and client organizations, and it provides practical exercises that walk participants through analyzing their own listening behavior, learning a step-by-step process for listening, and practicing specific listening techniques that can be used in a variety of situations. The training modules presented in the book challenge trainees to try strategies they may be unfamiliar with in a context that encourages flexibility while in a supportive learning environment.

A number of original and adapted structured experiences and instruments that were developed specifically for this book are included. Please feel free to adjust them to meet your needs and apply them to other aspects of your learning program, as many can be used for a wide range of training topics, such as supervisory skills, communication skills, and conflict management. Some may already be familiar to you, as there are many effective foundational activities around listening training that work so well, it's hard to imagine a listening skills workshop without them.

Many thanks to Mark Morrow at ASTD Press for the opportunity to write this book and for his support and encouragement throughout. I appreciate Mark's guidance, approachability, and way of putting me at ease. Thank you as well to Carol Field and her team at Aptara for making the editing process so smooth and stress-free, and for their diligence and professionalism in spotting changes that needed to be made.

I also thank Lisa Haneberg, friend, colleague, and ASTD author, for encouraging me to start writing and for her willingness to connect me with ASTD Press. Her resources helped jump-start this publishing journey for me, and for that, I am truly grateful. Thank you to my friends, family, and learning and development colleagues with ASTD Puget Sound and beyond who offered their support and enthusiasm for this endeavor. Special thanks as well to Coral Rice with The Growth Partnership, Inc., who provided me with the flexibility to write this book while balancing other priorities.

Finally, I offer my thanks to my husband, Chris, technical writer and proofreader extraordinaire, whose unwavering love and support with all of my adventures fuels the fire within.

Lisa J. Downs

Redmond, Washington

February 2008

◆

Introduction: How to Use This Book Effectively

- ◆ Practical definition of listening

- ◆ Discussion of common issues in teaching listening skills

- ◆ Explanation of how to use this workbook most effectively

What Is Listening?

The word *listening* is defined as making an effort to hear something; to pay attention or heed. It is different from *hearing*, which is the physiological process of the ear absorbing sound waves and transferring them along neural pathways to parts of the brain. Hearing is necessary for listening, but listening is much more than processing sound. Someone may hear very well but be a very poor listener.

Listening generally involves a five-step process: attending, understanding, interpreting, responding, and remembering. This process is active rather than passive and involves using a number of behaviors and tools to be most effective. The various types of listening—critical, empathic, informational, and appreciative—have their own characteristics and techniques. Which type of listening is used and which behaviors are involved depend on the situation and the people engaged in conversation. Self-awareness plays an important role in being a good listener. A large part of the facilitator's role for a listening skills workshop is to help learners recognize their strengths and weaknesses when it comes to listening and to help them develop strategies to increase their listening effectiveness.

For purposes of this workbook, *listening* is defined as paying close attention to someone's words and ideas.

Why This Is Important

Listening is an activity that may take many different forms for different people. The behaviors and tools used by someone in one listening situation may not be the same as those used in another. It is important, then, to emphasize this point when teaching effective listening skills. Although there is a process to follow to be an effective listener and certain behaviors lead to success more than others, learners may not use all of the techniques provided in a workshop. They may also use strategies in different ways to accomplish the same goal of improving their listening effectiveness, and this is perfectly acceptable. This book helps accelerate development and effective training to prepare participants to improve their listening skills and their overall communication with others.

How the Book Was Developed

The author reviewed available literature on effective listening training and combined this knowledge with her extensive experience in teaching listening skills, as well as in the design and delivery of effective, interactive training for adult learners. Having led numerous seminars in many aspects of interpersonal communication, she currently serves as a workshop facilitator and coach to help others improve their personal effectiveness.

The Context of the Training

The materials and designs in this book lend themselves to a broad array of organizations, both public and private. The training materials focus on helping participants be aware of their listening behaviors and then develop the skills necessary to be an effective listener. Although the book is designed to train people for one-on-one listening scenarios, with little or no adjustment, many of the approaches and principles also apply to small- or large-group listening situations.

The Content of the Training

The various aspects of listening, which include types, behaviors, nonverbal communication, and giving and receiving feedback, will be new information for many learners. Some participants or organizations, however, may not consider listening to be a skill that requires much training; they may take the stance that someone is either a good listener or a bad listener and there is not much that can be done about it. This viewpoint increases the difficulty of teaching listening skills for some trainers.

Another related issue in some organizations is the lack of resources, particularly time, to offer training of this nature. Other training topics, initiatives, or projects may take priority over effective listening. To help mitigate this issue, clearly identify and communicate the desired results of the training so participants and others in the organization understand the benefits and skills taught during an effective listening workshop.

The training designs in this workbook are intended to address these concerns. The content modules in chapter 10 are divided into basic skills required for effective listening and skills specific to particular ways of responding as a listener and engaging in conversation.

BASIC SKILLS

- ◆ **Content Module 10-1: Listening Buddies.** This module helps create a collaborative learning environment by introducing participants to each other, and suggests that their roles are to contribute to the learning process.

- ◆ **Content Module 10-2: Listening Defined.** The term *listening* may be ambiguous for many people. This module clarifies what it means to listen and the importance of identifying good listening.

- ◆ **Content Module 10-3: Listening Self-Assessment.** This module helps participants assess their strengths and weaknesses in terms of listening and explores how poor listening can negatively affect communication.

- ◆ **Content Module 10-4: The Listening Process.** The five-step process for effective listening is included in this module.

- ◆ **Content Module 10-5: Types of Listening.** This module explains the four most common types of listening and techniques for improvement of each type.

- ◆ **Content Module 10-6: Nonverbal Communication.** This module helps participants understand the messages nonverbal communication may send to a speaker and how to use nonverbal messages appropriately in effective listening.

- **Content Module 10-7: Effective Listening Behavior.** Positive and negative behaviors for listening are the focus for this module. Participants will explore the behaviors they currently exhibit and those they need to develop more effectively.

- **Content Module 10-8: The Bad Listener.** This module explores the many types of bad listening behaviors and how to recognize them. Participants also get firsthand experience in dealing with some bad listeners and strategies to deal with them.

RESPONDING SKILLS

- **Content Module 10-9: Paraphrasing.** This module provides participants with an opportunity to practice the technique of paraphrasing as a response to a speaker and to learn when paraphrasing may be a good option.

- **Content Module 10-10: Empathic Listening.** This module focuses on how to use empathic listening successfully, especially in highly emotional situations or when in conflict. One of the primary types of listening, empathic listening can be a tough skill to master.

- **Content Module 10-11: Giving and Receiving Feedback.** This module addresses how to give and receive feedback effectively, which is a critical aspect of being a good listener.

The Probable Realities of Participants

Most participants in a training course have common issues and common experiences. Although the needs-assessment process will provide specific information for a particular group of participants or for an organization, the following issues are present in many workshop situations. Being aware of these issues may help the trainer to design and facilitate a training program on effective listening.

- **Participants may not want to be in the training workshop.** Not all attendees want to be sitting in class, and some see it as a waste of their time, particularly if the training topic is on the soft side. All or some of the participants may have been told to be in the workshop as part of a mandatory curriculum.

- **Participants may not have a clear understanding of the desired results of the training.** Lack of clarity about the benefits of attending a workshop about effective listening, as well as the skills they will learn, may negatively affect learners' participation.

◆ **Participants may not have had any training on how to be a good listener.** Listening is often viewed as a naturally occurring skill. People are often told that they are good listeners or need to be better listeners, but they may be unclear about what that means and how to improve. It's a good sign that they are attending the workshop, but they may not have had any formal training on the topic prior to the program.

◆ **Some participants may not have time to practice their listening skills.** People often see the skills they learn in a workshop as an addition to their normal tasks and activities. In particular, some may feel that it will take more time during conversations to listen well, and that they just don't have the additional time every day. Although this could be the case, it may be that some participants have trouble seeing how they can incorporate new learning into their lives.

◆ **Participants may perceive attending the training as a sign that they are highly deficient in the skills being addressed.** If the training is mandatory for some participants, they may see this as an embarrassment based on their level of listening skills. This perception may or may not be true. Some people view training as a remedial activity rather than one designed to enhance personal and professional effectiveness. This attitude may affect participation in training exercises.

◆ **Participants come into the training with marked differences in their skill and knowledge levels.** A single workshop may contain participants from all levels in the organization's hierarchy with varying degrees of knowledge, skill, and experience. Those at the high end of the spectrum may think the workshop is not aligned with their experience level, and those at the more junior level may be intimidated to be in the same training as their supervisors or senior management.

◆ **Participants may not have any clear incentive to improve their listening skills.** Some training attendees may not be internally motivated to develop their listening skills, and there may not be any consequence, such as a negative score on a performance measure, for this. In these situations, the trainer may face resistance to participation in workshop activities or large-group discussion.

◆ **Need to listen effectively may be tied to increasing customer satisfaction.** For many participants, improving their listening skills may affect their relationships with their clients or customers, in turn leading to referrals and increases in status or compensation.

◆ **Participants have received a specific directive to improve their listening skills.** Some participants may attend the training to learn ways to address specific situations or issues with their listening skills. Although this could easily enhance the workshop, participants may attempt to steer discussion and activities toward helping them resolve a particular issue, which could inhibit the learning experience for others.

◆ **Participants may need to deal with competing interests during the training.** Whether it is checking voicemail, handling email, or dealing with an urgent client issue, some participants may not fully attend the workshop or may attempt to multitask during the listening skills training. This may affect the learning environment and the effectiveness of training activities, as well as the others' workshop experiences.

How to Use This Book

The best use of this resource is to develop and conduct training sessions to improve the listening skills of learners. Both experienced and novice trainers will be able to use this book in a flexible manner to ensure that their sessions meet the real needs of their client organizations.

Sample training designs are included in this book, along with the materials they require. The individual content modules, structured experiences, assessments, and training instruments can also be incorporated into training already offered, or they can be mixed and matched into a variety of custom designs.

The author strongly suggests that you

◆ Identify your target audience for effective listening training.

◆ Assess the learning needs of potential participants.

◆ Modify the enclosed designs, if necessary, or develop new ones.

◆ Evaluate the outcomes of the participants' training sessions to ensure their continuous improvement as trainers and of the training sessions.

This book can be a reference from which you borrow the structured experiences, instruments, assessments, and designs that fit your specific needs. A comprehensive set of steps that can help you get the most value out of this book appears at the end of this chapter under the heading "What to Do Next."

The Book's Organization

This resource contains numerous individual items that can be combined in many training designs for learners. Here are the major sets of materials:

- **Methods and effective practices** in assessing the learning needs of actual or potential participants (chapter 2).

- **Evaluation methods and effective practices** for effective listening sessions, including assessment of the trainer and continuous improvement approaches (chapter 5).

- **Content modules** that are either ready to use or that can be modified to meet specific needs (chapter 10).

- **Assessments and training instruments** that address several vital dimensions of listening effectiveness (chapter 11 and CD).

- **Structured experiences** on a variety of topics relevant to effective listening training (chapter 12 and CD).

- **Microsoft Word documents** to assist in customizing the participants' manuals (CD).

- **Microsoft PowerPoint presentations** to assist trainers in making presentations and giving instructions (CD).

- **Bibliography** of additional resources that can support effective listening training.

The goals of this book are to instruct and equip trainers with the tools to design and conduct listening training for learners that is highly interactive, engaging, and clearly on target.

Icons

Assessment: Appears when an agenda or learning activity includes an assessment, and it identifies each assessment presented.

CD: Indicates materials included on the CD accompanying this workbook.

Clock: Indicates recommended timeframes for specific activities.

Discussion Questions: Points out questions you can use to explore significant aspects of the training.

Handout: Indicates handouts that you can print or copy and use to support training activities.

Key Point: Alerts you to key points that you should emphasize as part of a training activity.

PowerPoint Slide: Indicates PowerPoint presentations and slides that can be used individually. These presentations and slides are on the CD that accompanies this workbook, and copies of the slides are included at the end of chapter 9. Instructions for using PowerPoint slides and the CD are in the appendix.

Structured Experience: Introduces structured experiences (participant exercises), which are included in chapter 12.

Training Instrument: Identifies specific tools, checklists, and assessments that are used before, during, and after the training workshop.

What to Do Next: Highlights recommended actions that will help you make the transition from one section of this workbook to the next, or from one specific training activity to another within a training module.

What to Do Next

♦   Study the entire contents of the book to get an overview of the resources it contains.

◆ Review the contents of the accompanying CD so that you can understand how it relates to the material in the printed book. Open the files in Microsoft Word, PowerPoint, and Adobe Acrobat Reader so you are able to determine how to make copies of the forms you will need to print and the presentations you may use to enrich the material. This step should include a careful reading of the document "How to Use the Contents of the CD," which is included on the CD.

◆ Study and apply the strategies outlined in chapter 2, "Assessing the Needs of Learners," to ensure that your sessions with learners are relevant and timely.

◆ When you have absorbed the information you discover in your training needs assessment, proceed to chapter 3. Design your session to meet the specific learning needs your potential participants have expressed. Carefully consider modifying the designs in this book as you formulate your plan for facilitating the learning of your client audience. You can use the sample designs in chapters 6 through 9 or modify them as your needs analysis suggests. The content modules in chapter 10 are detailed. You can plan to use them as they are or modify them. Chapters 11 and 12 contain the structured experiences, assessments, and training instruments the modules require. Because each of these is also a stand-alone item, you can easily incorporate any or all of them into your existing training designs.

◆ Prepare to facilitate your training by studying the approaches in chapter 4. Each of your sessions should improve on the previous ones, and that chapter contains tips on how you can make sure that you learn along with your trainees. You will learn to become a highly effective facilitator; the trainees will learn to become highly effective listeners.

◆ Plan to evaluate each of your training sessions. Chapter 5 tells you why this is important and gives you steps for gaining insight into the pay-offs of your listening training. Outline the steps you will take to gather and analyze evaluation data, and modify your training design as a result.

Assessing the Needs of Learners

- Methods for needs assessment

- Tips to improve your assessment

- How to use two key assessment tools

- Guidelines for conducting successful focus groups

Assessment Steps

A training needs assessment is the process of identifying how training can meet the needs of an organization and of learners. It serves as the foundation for a successful training program and supports employee performance with the ultimate goal of adding value to meet an organization's business needs. These are common steps in conducting a needs assessment:

- **Identify the business needs of the organization and determine its culture.** A needs assessment will help gauge whether a listening skills workshop is indeed a solution or there is some other underlying performance issue present in the organization. Sometimes, an organization may think training will cure all ills, and if so, an assessment will reveal this information. Ask such questions as: What business strategies would an effective listening training support? What business problems exist that listening skills training could help solve? What data exists that may provide insight into this business need? What measures will be used to determine whether the training has had an effect on the business?

◆ **Identify the performance and learner needs.** It's important to know what behaviors need to change to determine whether effective listening training is the appropriate solution. Data regarding potential learners' current and required performance, as well as their current and required skill and knowledge levels, will be helpful during this step in the needs-assessment process. Ask such questions as: What do learners need to stop or start doing differently? What are the learners' current levels of achievement with regard to being good listeners, and what should they be? What knowledge and skills should employees learn to be effective listeners? What are the learning styles of potential participants?

◆ **Analyze the data.** The data collected will reveal whether an effective listening skills workshop should be recommended and who should be in the training. Look at any gaps in performance, knowledge, and skills; then determine the best candidates for the training based on the needs of the learners and the organization.

◆ **Deliver recommendations.** Present the findings of the assessment, including training and nontraining recommendations (processes and procedures, environment and accountability). Share information regarding how the success of effective listening training will be measured, how the training will be designed and delivered, and how the program will be evaluated.

These methods and tools can help you complete the assessment process:

Methods

Many strategies determine what potential training participants need to learn. Some are more time-consuming than others, but here are five that are used frequently:

◆ **Existing Data.** This can include benchmarking reports, performance appraisals, strategic plans, competency models, financial reports, job descriptions, mission statements, and annual reports. This method has the advantages of being readily accessible from the organization and providing hard, reliable data and measures. Since this information is typically gathered for purposes other than training, it is necessary to make inferences from it to determine whether training issues are present.

- **Surveys.** Participants answer a series of focused questions, typically by a deadline; results are easy to tally and analyze. This method is usually an inexpensive way for respondents to provide information quickly and easily, either via an electronic tool or a paper-and-pencil questionnaire. It is important, however, to word the questions carefully so they yield the desired data, as well as mean the same thing to each respondent.

- **Interviews.** This includes one-on-one discussions, either face to face or over the phone, to gather data about individual learner and business needs. Plan interview questions ahead, record the session (with the interviewee's permission), and take notes. Although this is a time-consuming method, it can provide great detail and draw out information that is difficult to obtain from a survey. The interviewer must objectively record responses and not add his or her interpretation to what is said.

- **Focus Groups.** A facilitator conducts a group interview, which can provide information about learners' skill and performance levels, the work environment, culture, and perceptions of potential training participants. An advantage to this data-collection method is that all participants can hear and build on each other's ideas. It can also be time-consuming, and it may be beneficial to have more than one facilitator conduct a focus group session.

- **Observation.** The observer visits the organization to watch learners do their jobs, then records information regarding such items as behavior patterns, task performance, interactions with others, and use of time. Although this method is helpful to assess training needs and skill levels for individual learners, the observer cannot typically assess mental processes. Individuals may also behave differently around an observer than they would under normal circumstances.

Assessment Tips

Assessing the needs of learners should be carried out in a respectful, thoughtful way. Here are some tips that may help:

- **Gather the data that is going to provide an accurate and thorough assessment.** Discuss with the client what will be involved in conducting a needs assessment and the approach taken to gain buy-in. Be sure to collect the data that will get at the heart of the learners' and organization's needs regarding effective listening training, and go to the source(s) that will best be able to provide accurate, pertinent information.

◆ **Focus only on the training and nontraining needs you can provide.** A needs assessment can be a reflection of your competency, so be sure that you are able to deliver on all solutions that arise from assessment results, whether they include listening skills training, coaching, or helping to fix a breakdown in a process. Trainers need to be competent in a variety of learning and performance areas to conduct a thorough needs assessment for an organization. It is also in the best interests of the client to offer more than just a workshop as a possible solution to a performance or business issue.

◆ **Involve learners directly.** Ask learners about their needs through an interview, survey, or other assessment method; this is a simple way to gather important data and gain buy-in from potential training participants. Information about preferred learning styles, previous experiences with listening training, skill levels, and what they would like to learn in an effective listening workshop will enhance the design and delivery of the training, as well as signal to the learners that they play a direct role in influencing the content and activities in a training session.

◆ **Use a variety of data-collection methods.** Use two or three methods to ensure that the correct solution will become apparent and that the needs of the clients and learners will be met. This also helps avoid analysis paralysis and the possibility of getting bogged down by too many tools and too much information. Additionally, using different methods will help maintain reliability and objectivity throughout the needs-assessment process.

◆ **Present information free of trainer jargon.** Make an effort to address decision makers in language that is familiar to them rather than trainer or performance improvement jargon that may confuse or alienate them. As with other professions, the field of learning and development contains its own acronyms, as well as language that those outside of the discipline may not understand. Stick to a discussion of success, impact on business issues, strategy, and learner needs.

Two Key Resources

Chapter 11 of this workbook contains two useful tools that trainers can use to assess the developmental needs of learners. Adapt either or both according to the client's requirements.

- ◆ **Assessment 11–1: Learning Needs-Assessment Sheet.** This tool follows the steps in conducting a needs assessment and is designed to help you record information obtained by using the interview method of data collection. Adapt this form as needed. The Microsoft Word file is included on the CD that accompanies this workbook.

- ◆ **Assessment 11–2: Listening Self-Assessment.** Use this assessment as either a training tool or prework for an effective listening training session. You may also adapt the instrument for 360-degree assessments. Edit the Word file on the CD that accompanies this workbook.

Using Focus Groups in Training Needs Assessment

A focus group is an efficient method for gathering data on the learners' needs for an effective listening training session. It is best to have at least two facilitators conduct the focus group: one responsible for leading the session and keeping the group on track, and the other responsible for recording the information from the session. The facilitators may want to alternate performing the roles of facilitator and recorder, depending on the length of the session and the strengths of the facilitators. It is important to have an agenda for the session and monitor the flow of conversation, since participants may have a tendency to go off on tangents or begin complaining about a variety of subjects. It is also difficult to capture information when participants speak quickly, so it may be best to use audio or other equipment to record the conversation.

Here is a step-by-step process you can adapt to prepare for and conduct effective focus group sessions to assess the needs of learners:

- ◆ Determine the audience for effective listening training and collect the contact information for each person.

- ◆ Schedule well in advance one or two focus group sessions in private, easily accessible facilities. Allow at least an hour for each session.

- ◆ Invite the members of the target audience to attend one or more focus groups to discuss what they would like to gain from listening skills training, how improved listening could benefit communication in the organization, and the interpersonal communication challenges they face. Limit the group size to five or seven members to encourage participants to speak freely and to record the conversation efficiently.

◆ Print sufficient copies of "Assessment 11-3: Needs-Assessment Discussion Form" in chapter 11, and bring along extra supplies (such as pens, pencils, and notepads) for the participants.

◆ As the focus group begins, greet and welcome each person. Introduce yourself and ask participants to introduce themselves by sharing the following information. You may want to write this list on a flipchart or whiteboard:

  ◆ Name

  ◆ Job title

  ◆ Length of service at the organization

  ◆ How they would currently rate themselves as a listener on a scale from 1–10

  ◆ What their biggest challenge is when it comes to listening

◆ Share with the participants the purpose of the needs-assessment, how the data will be used, and why you were chosen to conduct the assessment. Ask their permission to record the focus group session.

◆ Hand out copies of "Assessment 11-3: Needs-Assessment Discussion Form," and ask the participants to complete it candidly. Be sure they do not put their names on the forms and explain that you will collect the sheets after the session.

◆ Ask the participants if they need more time, and when ready, explain that they can still make changes on the form during the discussion if they wish.

◆ Proceed around the room by asking question one on the form. Be sure that you understand what each person says, and don't be afraid to ask for clarification or examples, or to probe for specifics. It is also a good idea to paraphrase responses for the other members of the group. Encourage participants to share what they have in common in response to the question.

◆ Facilitate the group's discussion through the remaining questions on the form. Start with a different participant each time, and intervene if necessary if one group member starts to dominate the discussion.

◆ Summarize the common themes and ideas that came out of the discussion with the participants, and verify the accuracy of what was said.

◆ Collect the participants' discussion forms and remind them that the information will be used to help determine the content and activities for effective listening training that they will be invited to attend. If the training has been scheduled, share this information with the participants.

◆ Thank the focus group members for participating.

Designing Interactive Training

What's in This Chapter?

* Basic principles of adult learning

* Ideas for creating successful training sessions

* Training design tips

Principles of Design in Adult Learning

Good design is the essence of effective listening training and is a critical piece for meeting the needs of learners and the client organization. It requires careful thought about the readiness, learning styles, and training needs of potential workshop participants. An effective sequence of events must be created to ensure that people will learn what is required in the allotted timeframe. The facilitator needs to have a structured plan to help learners develop the knowledge, skills, techniques, and attitudes necessary for success. A solid training design will make the trainer more comfortable and better able to deliver an effective program that capitalizes on the facilitator's strengths and abilities as it addresses the participants' needs.

Malcolm Knowles (1998) has long been considered the father of adult learning and was the first to popularize the term *andragogy* to refer to the science of teaching adults. As a result of his thorough research about how adults learn, he identified several assumptions about adult learning that affect how training is designed. Here is a list of those principles and the implications for effective listening training design:

> * Adults need to know why they must learn something before they
>   learn it. It's the facilitator's responsibility, then, to explain why the

learning is of value and how the training will help improve their listening skills.

- ◆ Adults need to feel that others consider them to be capable of making their own decisions and directing their own lives. They may fear that training will be like their school experiences and thus resist participation. Trainers must create learning experiences that help adults make the transition from dependent to independent learners by providing them with useful strategies and tools.

- ◆ The richest resources for adult learning are the learners themselves. Adults all have unique experiences to share, as well as varied backgrounds, motivations, learning styles, interests, and needs. It will be most effective for the facilitator to use the participants' experiences with listening and communicating during the training session.

- ◆ Learning must be authentic, because adults are ready to learn to cope with real-life situations. It is also important that the learning coincide with a participant's development and be appropriate for the learner's skill and knowledge levels. Facilitators can ensure that the training meets the needs of all learners through a variety of structured experiences and shared information that directly address listening and interpersonal communication issues.

- ◆ Adults are motivated to learn if they believe that the training will help them on the job and in their relationships. The most effective training helps participants perform tasks and handle problems that they confront in their everyday lives. Participants in an effective listening training session should be allowed to influence the learning approach. Facilitators should use interactive training methods that focus on how participants can apply the learning and change their behavior.

- ◆ Adults are strongly motivated by internal pressures: quality-of-life issues, job satisfaction, or respect in the workplace. Each person's motivation type and level of are different, so it is up to the trainer to identify those motivators and decide the best way to incorporate them into the training, which can be challenging.

 Adult learners are goal-oriented, with little time and a finite capacity to absorb information. Limit lecture time for delivering information to allow a free exchange of ideas, and vary the presentation. This will also provide an engaging environment and ensure that different learning styles are considered.

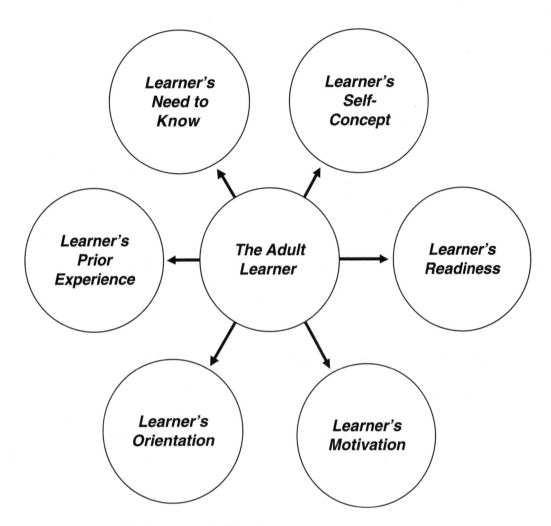

Figure 3.1 Adult Learning in Practice

Source: Knowles, Malcolm S., Elwood F. Holton III, and Richard A. Swanson. *The Adult Learner* (5th edition). Houston, TX: Gulf Publishing Company, 1998.

Give participants frequent breaks during a lengthy training session so they have opportunities to attend to their needs and get a mental break.

Figure 3.1 is a visual representation of Malcolm Knowles's elements of the adult learning model.

A Note on Training Language

The information about adult learning principles and their implications for designing effective listening training should make it clear that training is not teaching. Facilitators should not use language associated with education.

For each word below, facilitators should substitute the training language in parentheses:

- ◆ Course (training session)

- ◆ Instructor (facilitator)

- ◆ Evaluation (assessment)

- ◆ Classroom (training room, facility, or venue)

- ◆ Textbook (participant manual or guide)

 The organizational learning experience differs greatly from most academic experiences and is more targeted and practical. Many people have negative memories of their formal schooling, so trainers should be careful to avoid such reminders when they design training.

Using the Sample Designs in This Book

If you study the sample designs in chapters 6 through 9 and the content modules in chapter 10, you will discover a number of effective practices in designing interactive training for effective listening. Here are the major generalizations you may make in reviewing this material:

- ◆ **Break up the training into segments.** Determine the chunks of time you have, such as a half day or a full day.

- ◆ **Break each major segment into smaller chunks.** Design each chunk so it has a beginning, middle, and end, and structure the length of each segment according to the time required for each activity. Be sure to consider participant breaks, time to get organized, and time for the facilitator to refresh himself or herself.

- ◆ **Anticipate which training activities may take more or less time than expected.** It is always better to plan too many activities than not enough, but you may need to adjust the timing of structured experiences depending on the participation level of the learners. If an activity takes longer or goes more quickly than anticipated, prepare to adjust the timing of your remaining activities or insert another activity on the spot.

- ◆ **Make a seamless transition from one training activity to the following activity.** Create transition statements so learners see the connection between activities, as well as how each module relates to the next, so the training doesn't feel segmented. One example may be, "Paraphrasing is one technique we can use to respond when we are listening to another person. Let's take a look at another..." The relationships between segments may be obvious to the training designer, but meaningful transition statements will help point out these connections to the participants.

◆ **Allow plenty of time for activity debriefings.** The debriefing discussions after each activity are crucial for the participants to commit to change their behavior and apply what they are learning. They also help clarify information and are an effective way to gauge if the activity has been effective.

◆ **Create a detailed action plan for each session.** The sample action plans in this workbook provide models for you to consider. Sometimes the training design includes activities the facilitator and participants can do after the formal session.

◆ **Share the desired results for the training with the participants.** Present an overview of the desired outcomes for the training. Refer to these outcomes throughout the session as you transition between segments and activities, so learners see how the pieces fit together. This should be limited to three outcomes to be most effective.

◆ **Consider offering a follow-up session for participants.** Depending on the participants' and client organization's commitment and needs, plan a refresher session about a month or two after the training. During this meeting, you can facilitate a discussion of what worked well for the participants, what is still challenging for them, and what additional training they would like to attend.

Tips on Designing Effective Training

When designing a training session, developers use a structured process to guide them and ensure that the training is effective. This work is both an art and a science and reflects the designer's approach to adult learning.

A common process used for training design is represented by the acronym ADDIE, which represents each of the five steps in the process: *a*nalysis, *d*esign, development, *i*mplementation, and *e*valuation. Here is an explanation of this method:

- ◆ **Analysis.** Conduct a thorough needs assessment of the client organization and its learners (see chapter 2) to determine what the training issues are and what the desired results of the learning should be.

- ◆ **Design.** Decide how to present the training content to address the learners' needs according to results of your needs assessment and adult learning principles. Determine the sequencing of the training segments and structured activities during this step.

- ◆ **Development.** Create training materials, such as PowerPoint presentations, handouts, participant manuals, and instructions for activities. This workbook provides the materials you will need to conduct effective listening training sessions, so you may not need to spend much time on this step of the process.

- ◆ **Implementation.** Schedule the training session and handle any logistical details (book the facility, arrange catering, and make sure the materials and any necessary equipment are at the session). The facilitator must also market the training to potential participants and make any necessary changes to the content and materials.

- ◆ **Evaluation.** Assess whether the training has achieved the desired results and met the learners' needs. The different levels of evaluation are explained in more detail in chapter 5.

Because people usually remember the first and last things you say and do, it is important to pay attention to the beginning and ending activities in designing training. It's true that first impressions are critical for success and it can be difficult to recover from a poor start, so be sure to set yourself up for success. A strong ending will leave the participants feeling confident, informed, and excited to put what they have learned into practice. Emphasize a plan of action at the end of the session.

It's also a good idea to anticipate various problems that may occur, such as fire alarm interruptions, power outages, equipment failures, and domineering or difficult participants. A back-up plan will help the training session go smoothly and will minimize stress for the facilitator.

It may also be beneficial to solicit feedback about your training design from colleagues beforehand to gauge the flow of the session and the appropriateness of activities. Ask one or more observers to sit in on a training session to help provide information on what may need to be changed and how the training can be most effective.

Ultimately, the training should be beneficial for the participants, the client organization, and the facilitator. To achieve this, the facilitator must have solid information about learning needs and use resources carefully and to the fullest extent possible.

◆

Facilitating Listening Skills Training

- ◆ Definition of the facilitator role

- ◆ Strategies for engaging adult learners

- ◆ Techniques for capturing and holding trainees' attention

- ◆ Tips on creating a learning environment

The Role of the Facilitator

Facilitating training effectively combines the roles of event planner, public speaker, counselor, and entertainer.

- ◆ **Event planner.** The effective delivery of a training program requires careful coordination regarding facilities, equipment, materials, and participants. Contingency arrangements must be made for times when things don't go according to plan. Large training departments may provide administrative help with logistics planning, but when participants arrive, it's up to the facilitator to make sure everything is running smoothly. In larger groups, facilitation also involves crowd control. A big part of creating a productive learning environment includes making sure the participants are back from breaks on time and are refocused.

- ◆ **Public Speaker.** When you are the facilitator, the spotlight is on you. The participants depend on you for behavioral cues, and your physical presence and speaking style set the tone for the program. You need to know your material so you can convey it to others. Since anything can happen in interactive design, you must also be able to think and react quickly.

◆ **Counselor.** A facilitator's most important skill is the ability to be an active listener to the participants' verbal comments and physical cues, as well as to understand their concerns and questions. Listening intently for an extended period of time can be mentally exhausting, so be well rested and prepared. This emphasis on the listening role is perhaps the most critical difference between facilitators and the teachers most of us experienced as students.

◆ **Entertainer.** Few of us are good stand-up comedians (and we shouldn't try to be). Nevertheless, participants feed on the energy of the facilitator. A low-energy, soft-spoken, unanimated facilitator will create a low-energy program with little participant interaction. An engaging facilitator uses humor, interesting personal stories, sincere interest in the participants and subject matter, and—most important—high energy.

Although planning, effective speaking, listening, and demonstrating high energy increase the effectiveness of a facilitator, it is also important to be yourself. Emphasize your strengths and downplay skills or behaviors with which you are less comfortable. Don't try to be someone you're not. Use the materials in this book to design a training program well suited to your skills and personality.

What Is a Facilitator?

There can be confusion within the training and development field about the terminology used to denote people or roles. Here are some useful distinctions:

◆ **Facilitator.** From the French word "facile," which means "easy," facilitation is the art and science of assisting learners in experiencing content. Because the facilitator role is the subject of this chapter, this distinction will become clearer later. Facilitation typically occurs in organizational meetings and training sessions.

◆ **Educator.** This person teaches, or disseminates knowledge and understanding, to students or pupils. The educator, or teacher, operates in classroom and laboratory settings, leading students from a position of authority and superior knowledge. In training and development terms, many educators play the role of subject matter expert.

◆ **Trainer.** This role centers on helping trainees become competent in the areas in which they are working. The focal points are specific job-task knowledge, skills, and effective practices. Trainers typically operate in training rooms with groups of trainees.

◆ **Counselor.** Requiring specialized education and training, a counselor provides private, confidential assistance to employees with personal problems. Not all training and development practitioners are qualified to serve in this role.

◆ **Consultant.** With special emphasis on working with employees in a partnership arrangement, consultants help clients analyze situations that need attention, explore and evaluate options, and commit to action plans. There are two basic types of consultants: expert and process. Experts give clients advice; process-oriented consultants help clients learn how to improve work processes, including interpersonal ones.

The facilitator, then, works with learners in a manner that helps them open themselves to new learning and makes the process easy. The role requires the facilitator to set up activities that foster learning through hands-on experience and interaction. A common phrase used to define the facilitator's role is "to be the guide on the side and not the sage on the stage." Major aspects of excellence in facilitation include setting up proper experiential (participative) learning activities or exercises, as well as leading discussions of the results, referred to as debriefing. The structured experiences in chapter 12 contain instructions to facilitate debriefings. It's important to devote as much time to debriefing the exercises as to conducting them so participants will understand how they will apply the training content to their real-life experiences.

Engaging Adult Learners

When thinking about principles of adult learning (see chapter 3), include a variety of activities in effective listening training that will engage the learners and encourage their participation. Although it is often necessary to convey information through lecture, for example, by going through PowerPoint slides, a facilitator should spend no more than 15–20 minutes at a time on this type of presentation. The remainder of the time in each training module should focus on leading discussions, facilitating exercises, and otherwise engaging learners to make them active participants in the session.

Mixing the training methods used in a workshop provides variety for the facilitator and the learners; at the same time, it creates excellent opportunities for trainees to share their experiences, crystallize key concepts, and develop a plan of action for applying the content of the training to their everyday lives. Here are some common training methods that lead to participative learning:

- **Large-Group Discussion.** The facilitator poses questions to the full group of trainees; individual learners then respond to the questions in front of everyone, and others have the opportunity to add their ideas to the discussion. Each debriefing portion of the structured experiences in chapter 12 is meant to be a large-group discussion.

- **Small-Group Exercises.** Participants are divided into small groups (either by forming their own groups, numbering off, or a method chosen by the facilitator), in which they can have a discussion, a hands-on activity, a brainstorming session, or a problem-solving experience. Small groups usually have a time limit in which to complete their assignment, and one or more members of each group reports to the full group of trainees on what the group talked about, created, or decided.

- **Case Studies.** Here, learners are provided with detailed information about a real-life situation, including all circumstances, issues, and actions of people related to the case study. Participants, working either individually or in small groups, must analyze the case study, discuss, and share what was done well, what mistakes may have been made, and the implications for the topic at hand.

- **Role-Playing.** Some adult learners may hear the words "role play" and want to run for the nearest exit. Role playing, however, is a very effective way for participants to practice new skills, particularly for interpersonal communication, in a safe environment. Two or more trainees spontaneously dramatize a situation that relates to a problem. Each participant acts out a role as he or she feels it would be portrayed in real life. After the other learners observe the performance, a debriefing discussion is usually held to talk about the role play and its implications. Although some role plays are conducted in front of the large group, and others are done in small groups, everyone watches the debriefing portion. The facilitator needs to be sensitive to the different learners' personalities when conducting a large-group role play, since some may be uncomfortable performing in front of more than a handful of people.

- **Simulations.** A simulation is an abstract representation of a real-life situation that requires learners to solve complex problems. The facilitator creates aspects of the situation that are close to reality, and the learner must perform manipulations, respond, and take action to correct problems or maintain a certain status. Many simulations are computer controlled, for example, a flight simulator for airplane pilot training. After the training, the facilitator debriefs the learners and evaluates the results of the simulation.

◆ **Games.** A game is a formalized simulation activity. Two or more participants or teams compete with each other to meet a set of objectives that relate to a training topic. Set rules and procedures for the game include information that requires decision-making and follow-up actions. Typically, the facilitator handles the scoring and may give small trinkets as prizes for the winning participants or teams. Games can be played in small or large groups.

To engage adult learners and ensure that learning is participative, it is important to use a variety of training methods. Equally important, the facilitator should capture and hold the participants' attention. Part of the facilitator's role is to guard against boredom; here are some techniques for keeping the learners interested:

◆ Open with an introductory exercise that captures learners' attention and gets them engaged within the first 15 minutes of the training session. This helps set the tone and communicates to the participants that you value and encourage their involvement.

◆ Vary your rate of speech, volume, movement, facial expressions, and gestures. Although it is best to maintain a good volume to be easily heard and avoid distracting gestures and mannerisms, these subtle techniques can coordinate with what learners should attend to during the training.

◆ Break up explanations of key concepts with videos, demonstrations, examples, or readings from articles or books. This helps create memorable experiences for the participants and keeps things lively and interesting.

◆ Use appropriate and relevant humor, shock, suspense, or surprise. Share something unexpected, a funny anecdote, a startling statistic, or an applicable comic strip to engage learners and encourage discussion. These techniques provide good opportunities for trainees to identify with the content and explore different ideas.

Use Table 4–1 as a guide to help you decide what training methods to use and how to engage learners so their training experience is as participative and effective as possible.

Table 4–1

Selecting Instructional Methods and Tools

Choosing Training Methods

For each module, determine which of the following instructional methods you will use:

- ❑ Large-group discussion
- ❑ Small-group exercises
- ❑ Case studies
- ❑ Role-plays
- ❑ Simulations
- ❑ Games
- ❑ Lecture

Checking Training Design

For each module, make sure that you:

- ❑ Identify the learning objectives.
- ❑ Anticipate questions the participants may ask and formulate responses.
- ❑ Include enough exercises for learners to demonstrate knowledge and share past experiences.
- ❑ Provide correct responses (if applicable) and anticipate errors for each activity.
- ❑ Include activities that enable learners to share how they will apply content to their work.
- ❑ Allow sufficient time for debriefing discussions after exercises.

Logistics and Equipment

Check to be sure you have:

- ❑ Secured and tested necessary equipment to conduct the training.
- ❑ Produced ample copies of participant materials, assessments, and tools.
- ❑ Saved a back-up copy of your PowerPoint presentation.
- ❑ Secured (if applicable) and visited the training facility to assess the environment.

Other Issues to Consider

Have you provided an introductory activity that captures the attention of the learners within the first 15 minutes of the training?

❑ Yes　　　❑ No

Table 4–1, continued
Selecting Instructional Methods and Tools

Do you have a plan for minimizing distractions during the training and communicating this to the participants?

❑ Yes ❑ No

Have you practiced presenting the PowerPoint slides and conducting the activities in your training session?

❑ Yes ❑ No

Do you have a plan for how you will vary your actions and create memorable experiences for the learners during the training?

❑ Yes ❑ No

Adapted from: Carliner, Saul. *Training Design Basics*. Alexandria, VA: American Society for Training & Development, 2003.

Creating the Learning Environment

Creating a positive learning environment is a critical factor in making learning easy. The facilitator should seek to create four conditions to maximize learning:

- **Confidentiality.** The first step is to admit ignorance. Some trainees may fear the repercussions of showing their weaknesses. To alleviate these concerns, assure the participants that the sole purpose of the training is to build their listening and communication skills, and that no evaluations will take place. If discussions and events during the training program remain confidential among the participants and facilitators, this will help create a safe, risk-free environment.

- **Freedom from distractions.** Work and personal demands cannot be ignored during training, but they should be minimized as a courtesy to others; this will help each participant benefit from the training to the fullest extent possible. Ask that cell phones, personal digital assistants, and pagers be turned off or set to inaudible alerts. Selecting a training site away from the workplace will help reduce distractions greatly. Acknowledge that participants don't have time to be away from work but, inasmuch as they are, ask them to immerse themselves in the learning experience to get the most value from their training. Remind them also that they will have plenty of opportunities to check messages during breaks.

◆ **Participants are responsible for their own learning.** Experiential (participative) learning requires that trainees be actively engaged and committed to learning. The facilitator can only create the opportunity to learn; he or she cannot force anyone to learn. If a participant leaves a well-designed training session (which use of this book guarantees!) saying, "I learned nothing," then that statement reflects on the participant more than on the facilitator. The facilitator's role is to create a learning environment in which participants are challenged, intrigued, and able to explore and address their own developmental needs. It is up to the participants to respond to the learning environment and, if necessary, to inform the facilitator if the environment is not meeting their needs.

◆ **All participants are learning partners.** Each participant brings some relevant knowledge to the training program. A successful training session will tap into the knowledge of each participant through discussion and sharing of information. Encourage all participants to accept responsibility for helping others learn.

What to Do Next

◆ **Plan.** Make sure you are prepared to use all of the elements of your design effectively. Plan to maximize the appropriateness of your facilitation style. What will you be working on in your approach to training? What skills do you want to sharpen while facilitating this training? How will you obtain coaching and feedback on these skills?

◆ **Practice.** Go through the training materials in your design carefully. Be prepared to respond to trainees' questions that the materials and activities might generate. Present the PowerPoint slide shows to a friend or colleague to become more comfortable with the points you want to make.

◆ **Recruit co-facilitators.** You and your trainees can benefit from having co-facilitators, but it can be confusing and excessive to have more than two at once. An experienced manager or executive as co-facilitator means that you may need to coach the person to play the role of trainer. His or her active involvement can add greatly to the legitimacy of your training. Using subject matter experts, such as a well-known motivator or teacher, can also add depth and credibility to the delivery of your training. You will need to coach each of the subject matter experts before and after the session for maximum effectiveness and minimal surprises.

♦ **Prepare all needed materials and test your equipment.** Using the CD that accompanies this book, print enough copies of the assessments and training instruments needed in your design. Set up your computer to project the PowerPoint slide shows, and rehearse the ones called for by your design.

◆

Evaluating and Improving Listening Skills Training

What's in This Chapter?

- Overview of a classic training evaluation model

- How to use included instruments for your own training evaluation

- Tips on interpreting and making use of evaluation results

- Steps to successful evaluation

Why Bother?

Evaluating training can be extremely beneficial to both the trainer and the organization. Without an evaluation, you are essentially flying blind; you don't know whether the training is effective, whether participants learn anything during the training, or whether training has a positive effect on the organization.

Here are three motivations for, and benefits of, evaluating the listening skills training that you design and deliver:

1. The training outcomes should be aligned with the learning needs that you assessed earlier. In other words, did the training deliver on the needs that the learners in the organization have at the time?

2. You can justify the continuation of investing in listening skills and other training you provide if you can demonstrate that it is on target:

   - Did the learners like the training?

   - Did they learn the content?

   - Did they use the content?

   - Did it positively affect the organization's results?

3. By using a scientific approach to improve the design and delivery of the training you provide, you can demonstrate value to the organization by linking data to business decisions. Thoroughly evaluating listening skills training ensures that the continuous improvement of your training is driven by real information and not just by general impressions or anecdotes. It also conveys the message that you are serious about results, and it demonstrates your business acumen.

The Classic Levels of Training Evaluation

Donald Kirkpatrick (2006) developed a well-known model for training evaluation that consists of four levels; it guides much of the practice of measuring training outcomes in the learning and development field. The levels are graduated, from the relatively easy to measure to the more complex.

Level 1 – Reaction: Measuring the reaction of participants to the training. Although positive reactions may not ensure that learning takes place, negative reactions can certainly affect the likelihood of learning and whether the training will be offered again in the future.

Level 2 – Learning: Measuring the extent to which learning objectives have been achieved. Has knowledge increased? Have skills improved or attitudes changed as a result of the training?

Level 3 – Behavior: Measuring the extent to which participants changed their behavior in the organization because they attended the training.

Level 4 – Results: Measuring the organizational results from behavioral changes that were achieved because participants attended the training.

The least powerful, but most common, evaluation method is at the first level; they are brief reaction surveys commonly called Smile Sheets, which usually use Likert scales to measure the effectiveness of the training content and delivery, and usually include space to write comments. The questions are often about value and participant enjoyment of the training. Smile Sheets indicate immediate reactions of participants, but they may have no correlation to actual learning. An entertaining facilitator, comfortable learning environment, and good food can produce positive survey results, but it may not affect application of learning and behavior change. Some participants also follow the old adage, "If you can't say anything nice, don't say anything at all." They either give high scores that don't reflect their real reactions or they don't complete the evaluation. The participants may be more concerned with leaving the training facility and beating rush hour traffic than providing helpful feedback.

Smile Sheets are commonly used because they are easy to administer and can provide some value. Positive scores may not be indicative of effective training, but negative evaluations are a strong indication that the training is ineffective. Also, open-ended questions that allow participants to provide comments on the training can offer important, useful feedback.

Because the four evaluation levels are ranked according to complexity, they are also, in effect, ranked according to decreasing use. Due to ease of use, more organizations use Smile Sheets to evaluate training rather than attempt to measure learning and impact at the other three levels. Some may track learning by conducting pretests and posttests to assess skill level, but this may be limited to IT training subjects in many organizations. Fewer track behavior changes, and still fewer engage in the difficult task of measuring business results or return-on-investment for learning programs. The author strongly recommends that trainers take whatever steps they need to evaluate their sessions more thoroughly. If training is to be considered a key business activity, trainers need to be accountable for the value they claim to add to the organization and the effect on results.

Instruments for Evaluation in This Workbook

Chapter 11 of this workbook includes four instruments that lend themselves to applications of evaluating training. Some can also be used in training designs.

- **Assessment 11–2: Listening Self-Assessment.** This tool calls for listening skills training participants to analyze their strengths and developmental needs. The instrument can be used as prework for an initial training module, as well as a repeat measure either at the end of the session or sometime afterward.

- **Assessment 11–4: Facilitator Competencies.** This form helps establish learning priorities for your own development as a workshop facilitator. It can be used as a self-assessment or as a follow-up questionnaire to solicit feedback from trainees after a session or at a later time.

- **Assessment 11–5: Listening Skills Follow-Up Assessment.** Distribute this questionnaire some time after the end of the listening skills training. Targeting Level 3 of Kirkpatrick's training evaluation model, it can be used in follow-up reunions of trainees or as a survey. It can also include ratings from colleagues or supervisors in the participants' work environments.

◆ **Assessment 11–6: Training Evaluation.** Use this form to conduct a Level 1 Smile Sheet evaluation. It allows training participants to provide reaction feedback for the workshop and the facilitator.

Trainers are not limited to using these four instruments, of course. It is important to commit yourself to systematic evaluation and to conduct it routinely. In this way, you build up an understanding of what works best with your trainees and communicate your value to the client organization.

Improving Listening Skills Training

For many organizations, the concept of continuous improvement is of critical importance. As a training professional, it is in your best interest to demonstrate your attention to detail, as well as how you achieve the desired results. Be proactive to set yourself up for success; this will enable you to meet the needs of the organization and its learners in the best way possible.

Applied to listening skills training, commitment to continuous improvement means:

◆ Specify the steps you are taking.

◆ Analyze the logic of the sequence.

◆ Look carefully at the effectiveness of each step.

◆ Make changes that offer chances to make the training better.

This approach requires documentation and careful evaluation of the effects, or outcomes, of each step.

Pay close attention to clients' needs to provide work of high quality to organizations. In training, this means assessing the learning needs and preferences of potential participants, involving them in evaluating the training, and providing other services to them—such as one-on-one coaching—as they apply what they learn to their everyday work.

Trainers should avoid using their favorite learning activities; they should be more flexible and adapt to different organization and learner needs. A better approach to improving training is to experiment with both the content and design of the session. If activities do not produce desired results, either change or discontinue them. Try new ways and new activities to deliver the same learning objectives.

Learn ways to evaluate training on more than one of Kirkpatrick's levels, as well. The data gleaned from using Levels 2 through 4 of the model can provide great insight into how to improve your listening skills training. This is more time-consuming than simply distributing a Smile Sheet, but the pay-off can be substantial.

When time has passed after your training, you can also solicit feedback on your competence as a trainer and facilitator. This information can guide you through the process of developing as a learning professional. The root cause of less-than-optimal listening skills training is often the trainer, not the design. You may be interfering with the effectiveness of your sessions. Asking for feedback on what you can change is a direct way to manage your growth as a trainer, but soliciting honest feedback may not be a natural, comfortable thing for some people to do. You can become a role model for other trainers by actively engaging learners in your own quest for excellence.

What to Do Next

Here is a step-by-step method for maximizing the benefits of your efforts in evaluating your listening skills training sessions:

- **Decide which steps to follow.** Lay out a step-by-step plan for evaluating the outcomes (impacts, pay-offs) of your listening skills training. Specify who will do what, when, how much, and for what purpose. Establish a timeline for these steps.

- **Gather feedback.** Solicit data from trainees and any other relevant people. Use the instruments included in this book to assist you in this process.

- **Analyze results.** Conduct both statistical and content analyses of the responses you receive while gathering data for your evaluation. Be as objective as possible during this step because you may be predisposed to use the data to validate your own opinions and observations.

- **Modify the design as necessary.** Your evaluation program is the beginning of your design improvement process. Use the results to strengthen what works well, and change the selection, content, or sequence of activities to reach your training objectives more effectively.

◆

Individual and Small-Group Sessions

- ◆ Advice on working with individuals and small groups
- ◆ Considerations in choosing the right content for training sessions
- ◆ Step-by-step preparation and training delivery instructions
- ◆ Sample agendas

The materials in this workbook are designed to meet a variety of training needs. They cover a range of topics related to listening skills training and can be offered in many different formats and timeframes. Although it is possible to enhance learning experiences and increase their depth by lengthy immersion in the learning environment, organizational realities sometimes call for training to be done in short, small doses. Organizational size and work demands may also limit the number of participants available at any particular time. This chapter discusses session designs for listening skills training individually and in small groups.

Individual Session

TRAINING OBJECTIVES

The objectives of an individual training session are to convey as much information as possible to the participant in a short time, as well as to build the one-on-one relationship between the trainer and the participant. This interaction between trainer and participant is the greatest advantage of individual training sessions. The participant's specific questions and issues can be explored in greater depth than in a session with multiple participants.

An individual training session is appropriate for the following circumstances:

◆ The targeted, available audience for training is one person.

◆ One individual requires training in one particular area of content.

◆ Training facilities for multiple participants are not available.

 Time

◆ 1 to 2.5 hours

Choosing the Content

One of the advantages of training a single participant is the ability to select content specifically for an individual's needs. Although all of the content modules in this book can be used for individual training, some are more easily tailored than others. The structured experiences in this book typically require multiple participants, but some exercises may be executed by a single participant working with a trainer. The content modules most appropriate for an individual training session are:

◆ Content Module 10–2: Listening Defined

◆ Content Module 10–3: Listening Self-Assessment

◆ Content Module 10–4: Types of Listening

◆ Content Module 10–5: The Listening Process

◆ Content Module 10–6: Nonverbal Communication

◆ Content Module 10–7: Effective Listening Behavior

◆ Content Module 10–9: Paraphrasing

◆ Content Module 10–10: Empathic Listening

These modules are in chapter 10.

Not all of the modules are readily adaptable to individual training sessions, but there is enough content suitable for one-on-one training to cover a wide range of listening skills issues. Your training needs assessment will help you prioritize and select the content modules best suited to your audience.

The timing of certain topics is another thing to consider when choosing content. For instance, the "Listening Defined" module introduces us to the concept of listening, and provides a foundation for the other modules. It should be offered first if a series of modules will be presented. The "Listening Self-Assessment" module helps to focus the learning efforts of the trainee and should be offered early in the training process. The "Types of Listening" and "The Listening Process" modules help the learner understand ways to listen depending on the situation, and these modules provide the learner with a specific process to listen effectively. They are ideally offered before the "Non-verbal Communication," "Effective Listening Behavior," "Paraphrasing," and "Empathic Listening" modules.

The sample agenda is designed for someone who is beginning his or her training on listening. It contains the "Listening Defined" and "Listening Self-Assessment" modules.

Materials

For the instructor:

- This chapter for reference

- Content Module 10–2: Listening Defined

- Content Module 10–3: Listening Self-Assessment

- Structured Experience 12–1: Listening Buddies (with trainer acting as participant's partner)

- PowerPoint presentation: Listening Defined. To access slides for this program, open the file *Listening Defined.ppt* on the accompanying CD. Copies of the slides for this training session are included at the end of chapter 9 (slides 9–1 through 9–10).

For the participant:

- Assessment 11–2: Listening Self-Assessment

- Writing instruments

Sample Agenda

8:00 a.m.   Introductions (5 minutes)

8:05   Content Module 10–2: Listening Defined (chapter 10) (1 hour)

9:05	Break (10 minutes)
9:15	Content Module 10–3: Listening Self-Assessment (chapter 10) (1 hour)
10:15	Close

Step-by-Step Planning

At the training session:

- Introduce yourself to the participant. Include a description of your role in the training process, as well as your training and work experience. First impressions count, and this is your chance to establish credibility with the participant.

- Ask the participant to introduce himself or herself to you, including name, role, and what the participant would like to gain from the training. Let the participant know this is an informal session and try to put him or her at ease.

- Review the agenda and learning objectives with the participant.

- Go through the selected content module(s).

- Take a break about an hour into the session.

- Ask for questions and test for understanding frequently.

- Close the session with an opportunity for the participant to ask questions. If appropriate, offer your help and availability on an ongoing basis.

Small-Group Session

TRAINING OBJECTIVES

The objectives of a small-group training session are to convey as much information as possible to the participants in a short period of time, as well as to build a relationship between the trainer and the participants. The small-group setting allows in-depth discussion of a limited set of issues.

A small-group training session is appropriate for these circumstances:

- The targeted training audience consists of seven people or less.

- A few individuals require training in one particular area of content.

- Training facilities for large groups are not available.

Time

- 1 hour to 2 hours, 30 minutes

Choosing the Content

Any of the content modules in this book can be used for small-group training. Select the module(s) based on the needs assessment of the particular group.

This sample agenda assumes that the most pressing need for this small group is to have a model they can use to improve their listening skills. I've selected the "Participant Introductions" and "The Listening Process" modules. The former module is an introduction exercise that helps create the learning environment by preparing the participants to act as learning partners and share commonalities when it comes to their listening skills. The latter module helps participants use a process with specific steps to help them listen more effectively, and it provides them with an opportunity to practice careful listening and explore their own listening behavior.

Materials

For the instructor:

- This chapter for reference

- Content Module 10–1: Participant Introductions

- Content Module 10–5: The Listening Process

- Structured Experience 12–4: Having a Ball

- Structured Experience 12–5: Memorize This

- Training Instrument 11–1: Memory Game Word Lists

- Tennis or other medium-sized rubber balls for small groups

- PowerPoint presentation: The Listening Process. To access slides for this program, open the file *The Listening Process.ppt* on the accompanying

CD. Copies of the slides for this training session are included at the end of chapter 9 (slides 9–21 through 9–38).

For the participants:

◆   Writing instruments/blank paper

Sample Agenda

8:00 a.m.   Content Module 10–1: Participant Introductions (chapter 10) (15 minutes)

8:15   Content Module 10–5: The Listening Process (chapter 10) (2 hours, 15 minutes)

10:30   Close

Step-by-Step Planning

Just before the training session:

◆   Arrive early at the facility.

◆   Set up and test equipment (for example, laptop, projector, flipcharts).

At the training session:

◆   Introduce yourself to the participants. Include a description of your role in the training process, as well as your training and work experience. First impressions count, and this is your chance to establish credibility with the participants.

◆   If you do not use the introductory exercise, ask the participants to introduce themselves by sharing their names, roles, and what they would like to gain from the training. Let them know they will be helping each other learn.

◆   Review the agenda and learning objectives with the participants.

◆   Go through the selected content module(s).

◆   Take a break about an hour into the session.

◆   Ask for questions and test for understanding frequently.

◆ Close the session with an opportunity for the participants to ask questions. If appropriate, offer your help and availability on an ongoing basis.

What to Do Next

◆ Identify the training participant(s) and assess their most critical training needs.

◆ Determine the time available for the training session.

◆ Select the highest value content module(s) based on needs and time available.

◆ Schedule the session.

◆ Arrange a facility for the training session.

◆ Invite the participant(s).

◆ Send a confirmation to participant(s). Include an agenda and any advance work with the confirmation.

◆ Prepare training materials (handouts, overheads, and presentations).

◆

Half-Day Session

- ◆ Advice on choosing the content for training sessions

- ◆ Step-by-step preparation and training delivery instructions

- ◆ Sample agendas

The materials in this book can be used for a variety of training needs and timeframes. This chapter covers designs suitable for half-day (four-hour) training sessions. Since group training is generally more effective and enjoyable than one-on-one training sessions, try to use it whenever possible. Contributions from a variety of participants in a group enhances the learning environment. Although group learning dynamics can be achieved with only three participants, a group of between 12 and 24 participants is best.

Objectives and Use

The objectives of a half-day training session are to build understanding of the learning content that is of greatest value to the organization and the participants, and to build relationships between the trainer and the participants. The group setting allows for rich and diverse discussion of the various topics.

A half-day training session is appropriate for these circumstances:

- ◆ The targeted, available audience for training is three participants or more.

- ◆ The targeted audience requires training in several content areas.

◆ Training facilities for groups are available.

◆ The time available for the training session is limited to four hours.

Choosing the Content

Any of the content modules in this book can be used for half-day training sessions. Select the modules based on the needs assessment of the participant group. If the participant group has not identified a set of assessed needs (for example, if an assessment was not completed or an open registration process is being used), select the modules based on the competencies the organization seeks to develop.

Consider the order of certain topics when selecting which content will be offered first. As noted in the previous chapter, use the "Listening Defined" and "Listening Self-Assessment" modules early in the training process. The sample designs in this chapter include these modules in the first of several half-day sessions that together cover all of the book's content modules.

Note: When your training session is at least a half day long, you've crossed the refreshment threshold. Hunger and thirst are enemies to the learning environment, so offer beverages and snacks at the breaks so your participants' biological needs are met.

For the first sample agenda, we've selected the "Participant Introductions," "Listening Defined," and "Listening Self-Assessment" modules.

Sample Agenda One

The "Participant Introductions" module is an introduction exercise that helps create the learning environment; it prepares the participants to act as learning partners and share common characteristics of their listening skills. The "Listening Defined" module introduces us to the concept of listening, and sets the foundation for the rest of the listening skills training. The "Listening Self-Assessment" module helps participants recognize learning opportunities that offer the greatest leverage for improving their listening skills.

 ## Time

◆ 2 hours, 45 minutes

Materials

For the instructor:

- ◆ Content Module 10–1: Participant Introductions

- ◆ Content Module 10–2: Listening Defined

- ◆ Content Module 10–3: Listening Self-Assessment

- ◆ Structured Experience 12–1: Listening Buddies

- ◆ PowerPoint presentation: Listening Defined. To access slides for this program, open the file *Listening Defined.ppt* on the accompanying CD. Copies of the slides for this training session are included at the end of chapter 9 (slides 9–1 through 9–10).

For the participants:

- ◆ Assessment 11–2: Listening Self-Assessment

- ◆ Writing instruments

Sample Agenda

8:00 a.m.   Content Module 10–1: Participant Introductions (chapter 10) (30 minutes; varies by class size)

              Objective: Prepare participants to help each other learn.

8:30   Content Module 10–2: Listening Defined (chapter 10) (1 hour)

              Objective: Understand what listening is, the importance of properly defining *listening*, and its behaviors.

9:30   Break (10 minutes)

9:40   Content Module 10–3: Listening Self-Assessment (chapter 10) (1 hour)

              Objective: Identify each participant's highest-impact learning opportunities.

10:40   Close (5 minutes)

              Objective: Reinforce learning points.

10:45   Participants dismissed

Sample Agenda Two

Including breaks, this design extends slightly past the four-hour mark. The "Types of Listening" module helps participants learn about the four primary types of listening and gives tips for using each of them. There is also the opportunity to practice two of the types in the learning environment. The "Nonverbal Communication" module looks at the important role nonverbal communication plays in listening; it includes discussion of the different categories of nonverbals and tips for effective nonverbal communication.

Time

- ♦ 4 hours, 5 minutes

Materials

For the instructor:

- ♦ Content Module 10–4: Types of Listening Module
- ♦ Content Module 10–6: Nonverbal Communication
- ♦ Structured Experience 12–2: What's That Sound?
- ♦ Structured Experience 12–3: Newsworthy Note-Taking
- ♦ Structured Experience 12–6: Nonverbal Nonsense
- ♦ Structured Experience 12–7: Culture Shock
- ♦ Newspaper article of medium length

- ♦ PowerPoint presentation: Types of Listening. To access slides for this program, open the file *Types of Listening.ppt* on the accompanying CD. Copies of the slides for this training session are included at the end of chapter 9 (slides 9–11 through 9–20).
- ♦ PowerPoint presentation: Nonverbal Communication. To access slides for this program, open the file *Nonverbal Communication.ppt* on the accompanying CD. Copies of the slides for this training session are included at the end of chapter 9 (slides 9–39 through 9–46).

For the participants:

- ♦ Handout 12–1: Emotion Word Slips
- ♦ Handout 12–2: Cultural Differences in Nonverbal Communication
- ♦ Writing instruments/blank paper

Sample Agenda

8:00 a.m.   Content Module 10–4: Types of Listening (chapter 10) (2 hours)

Objective: Understand the primary types of listening and tips for using each of them to listen effectively.

10:00   Break (15 minutes)

10:15   Content Module 10–6: Nonverbal Communication (chapter 10) (1.75 hours)

Objective: Understand the importance of nonverbal communication when listening.

12:00   Close (5 minutes)

Objective: Reinforce learning points.

12:05   Participants dismissed

Sample Agenda Three

This agenda covers "The Listening Process" and "Effective Listening Behavior" modules. "The Listening Process" module helps participants use a process with specific steps to help them listen more effectively, and it provides them with an opportunity to practice careful listening and explore their own listening behavior. The "Effective Listening Behavior" module gives participants the opportunity to practice separating fact from inference.

Time

◆ 3 hours, 50 minutes

Materials

For the instructor:

◆ Content Module 10–5: The Listening Process

◆ Content Module 10–7: Effective Listening Behavior

◆ Structured Experience 12–4: Having a Ball

◆ Structured Experience 12–5: Memorize This

- Structured Experience 12–8: Fact or Fiction?

- Training Instrument 11–1: Memory Game Word Lists

- Tennis or other medium-sized rubber balls for small groups

- PowerPoint presentation: The Listening Process. To access slides for this program, open the file *The Listening Process.ppt* on the accompanying CD. Copies of the slides for this training session are included at the end of chapter 9 (slides 9–21 through 9–38).

- PowerPoint presentation: Effective Listening Behavior. To access slides for this program, open the file *Effective Listening Behavior.ppt* on the accompanying CD. Copies of the slides for this training session are included at the end of chapter 9 (slides 9–47 through 9–53).

For the participants:

- Handout 12–3: Argument Analysis

- Writing instruments/blank paper

Sample Agenda

8:00 a.m.   Content Module 10–5: The Listening Process (chapter 10) (2 hours, 15 minutes)

            Objective: Understand a process to use for listening with specific steps for greater effectiveness.

10:15   Break (15 minutes)

10:30   Content Module 10–7: Effective Listening Behavior (chapter 10) (1 hour, 15 minutes)

            Objective: Learn general principles and techniques to be an effective listener, including separating fact from generalization.

11:45   Close (5 minutes)

            Objective: Reinforce learning points.

11:50   Participants dismissed

Sample Agenda Four

This agenda contains two modules: "The Bad Listener" and "Paraphrasing."

Time

◆ 2 hours, 45 minutes

Materials

For the instructor:

◆ Content Module 10–8: The Bad Listener

◆ Content Module 10–9: Paraphrasing

◆ Structured Experience 12–9: Driven to Distraction

◆ Structured Experience 12–10: Paraphrasing Partners

◆ PowerPoint presentation: The Bad Listener. To access slides for this program, open the file *The Bad Listener.ppt* on the accompanying CD. Copies of the slides for this training session are included at the end of chapter 9 (slides 9–54 through 9–59).

◆ PowerPoint presentation: Paraphrasing. To access slides for this program, open the file *Paraphrasing.ppt* on the accompanying CD. Copies of the slides for this training session are included at the end of chapter 9 (slides 9–60 through 9–69).

Sample Agenda

8:00 a.m.   Content Module 10–8: The Bad Listener (chapter 10) (1 hour)

   Objective: Explore the many types of bad listening behaviors and how to recognize them.

9:00   Break (10 minutes)

9:10   Content Module 10–9: Paraphrasing (chapter 10) (1 hour, 30 minutes)

   Objective: Understand the elements and techniques of paraphrasing, one of many helpful listening techniques.

10:40   Close (5 minutes)

   Objective: Reinforce learning points.

10:45   Participants dismissed

Sample Agenda Five

This agenda contains the remaining modules, "Empathic Listening" and "Giving and Receiving Feedback."

Time

- ◆ 3 hours, 45 minutes

Materials

For the instructor:

- ◆ Content Module 10–10: Empathic Listening

- ◆ Content Module 10–11: Giving and Receiving Feedback

- ◆ Structured Experience 12–11: Empathic Listening Practice

- ◆ Structured Experience 12–12: Fun With Feedback

- ◆ PowerPoint presentation: Empathic Listening. To access slides for this program, open the file *Empathic Listening.ppt* on the accompanying CD. Copies of the slides for this training session are included at the end of chapter 9 (slides 9–70 through 9–79).

- ◆ PowerPoint presentation: Giving and Receiving Feedback. To access slides for this program, open the file *Giving and Receiving Feedback.ppt* on the accompanying CD. Copies of the slides for this training session are included at the end of chapter 9 (slides 9–80 through 9–91).

For the participants:

- ◆ Assessment 11–7: Feedback Self-Assessment

- ◆ Training Instrument 11–2: Empathic Listening Observation Checklist

- ◆ Training Instrument 11–3: Feedback Observation Worksheet

- ◆ Handout 12–4: Feedback Role-Play Scenarios

- ◆ Writing instruments

Sample Agenda

8:00 a.m.   Content Module 10–10: Empathic Listening (chapter 10) (1 hour, 30 minutes)

Objective: Learn a common listening technique that is especially effective in diffusing emotionally charged situations or dealing with conflict.

9:30   Break (10 minutes)

9:40   Content Module 10–11: Giving and Receiving Feedback (chapter 10) (2 hours)

Objective: Learn principles and techniques for giving and receiving feedback effectively.

11:40   Close (5 minutes)

Objective: Reinforce learning points.

11:45   Participants dismissed

Step-by-Step Planning

Just before the training session:

- ◆ Arrive early at the facility.

- ◆ Set up and test equipment (for example, laptop, projector, flipcharts).

- ◆ Confirm refreshments.

At the training session:

- ◆ Introduce yourself to the participants. Include a description of your role in the training process and your training and work experience. First impressions count, and this is your chance to establish credibility with the participants.

- ◆ If you do not use the participant introduction exercise, ask the participants to introduce themselves by sharing their names, roles, and what they would like to gain from the training. Let them know they will be helping each other learn.

- ◆ Review the agenda and learning objectives with the participants.

- ◆ Go through the selected content modules.

- ◆ Ask for questions, and test for understanding frequently.

- ◆ Close the session with an opportunity for the participants to ask questions. If appropriate, offer your help and availability on an ongoing basis.

At the second through fifth sessions:

- Review the agenda and learning objectives with the participants.

- Go through the selected content modules.

- Ask for questions, and test for understanding frequently.

- Close the session with an opportunity for the participants to ask questions. If appropriate, offer your help and availability on an ongoing basis.

What to Do Next

- Identify the training participants. Assess their most critical training needs, or identify the competencies the organization seeks to develop.

- Determine the agenda using the highest value content modules based on your needs assessment or the required competencies.

- Schedule the session.

- Arrange a facility for the training session.

- Invite participants.

- Send a confirmation to participants. Include an agenda and any prework with the confirmation.

- Prepare training materials (handouts, overheads, presentations, and exercise materials).

- Order food and beverages.

◆

Full-Day Session

What's in This Chapter?

- ◆ Advice on choosing the content for training sessions

- ◆ Step-by-step preparation and training delivery instructions

- ◆ Sample agendas

The materials in this book have been designed to meet a variety of training needs and timeframes. This chapter covers designs suitable for full-day (six-to eight-hour) training sessions.

Full-day training experiences, and those that are even longer, might raise concerns that participants will be overloaded with information. Nevertheless, the benefits of extended learning experiences can outweigh the potential drawbacks. A shorter program might be seen as part of a typical workday, but a longer program can become a memorable life experience for the participant, especially if it is held at an off-site venue. It often takes a different physical environment and a complete break from daily routine for participants to focus on learning. Creating the learning environment discussed in chapter 4 is easier in extended programs in which the various listening skills competencies can be thoroughly explored. Full-day sessions are appropriate for group training. The learning environment is enhanced by the backgrounds and experiences of a variety of participants. For full-day sessions, a group of between 12 and 24 participants is the most conducive to a learning environment.

Although this chapter includes illustrative designs, the trainer should adapt them to fit the training purposes. Each design can be modified to take into account the resources available, the learning readiness of potential participants, and, above all, the assessed development needs of the learners and the organization.

Objectives and Use

The objectives of a full-day training session are to free participants from their daily routine so they can understand the learning content that is of greatest value, as well as to build relationships between the trainer and the participants. The group setting allows for rich and diverse discussion of the various topics.

A full-day training session is appropriate for the following circumstances:

◆ The targeted, available audience for training is 12 participants or more.

◆ The targeted audience requires training in several content areas.

◆ Training facilities for groups are available.

◆ A full day is available for the training session.

◆ Funding for meals (and optionally) for an off-site location is available.

Choosing the Content

Any of the content modules in this book can be used as part of a full-day training session. Select the modules based on the needs assessment of the participant group. If the needs have not been identified for the group (either an assessment was not completed, or an open registration process is being used), select the modules based on the competencies the organization seeks to develop.

As noted for half-day sessions, the entire curriculum contained in this book also can be offered in a series of full-day sessions.

 When your training session is at least a full day long, you've crossed over the meal threshold. Hunger and thirst are enemies to the learning environment, so offer beverages and snacks at the breaks so your participants' biological needs are met. Lunch for participants is strongly suggested. Keep participants together during the lunch break to encourage continuing discussion of learning points. This also helps to strengthen the relationships among participants and, therefore, helps support the learning environment. In addition, a

scheduled lunch discourages participants from going back to the office and getting distracted from their learning focus. Finally, providing lunch helps to keep your session on schedule because participants are less likely to come back late from the lunch break.

Three sample agendas are included. Each is designed as a stand-alone training session and reflects a different major training issue pertaining to listening skills.

Sample Agenda One

This agenda reflects a requirement for training about basic listening skills and how participants can learn by following a specific process. This may have been identified as an organizational competency or as a common need for the participants. The timing of "The Listening Process" module assumes that both structured experiences for the module are conducted and the exact allocation of time is up to the workshop facilitator.

Time

- ◆ 7 hours, 30 minutes

Materials

For the instructor:

- ◆ Content Module 10–1: Participant Introductions

- ◆ Content Module 10–2: Listening Defined

- ◆ Content Module 10–4: Types of Listening

- ◆ Content Module 10–5: The Listening Process

- ◆ Structured Experience 12–1: Listening Buddies

- ◆ Structured Experience 12–2: What's That Sound?

- ◆ Structured Experience 12–3: Newsworthy Note-Taking

- ◆ Structured Experience 12–4: Having a Ball

- ◆ Structured Experience 12–5: Memorize This

- ◆ Training Instrument 11–1: Memory Game Word Lists

- ◆ Newspaper article of medium length

♦ Tennis or other medium-sized rubber balls for small groups

♦ PowerPoint presentation: Listening Defined. To access slides for this program, open the file *Listening Defined.ppt* on the accompanying CD. Copies of the slides for this training session are included at the end of chapter 9 (slides 9–1 through 9–10).

♦ PowerPoint presentation: Types of Listening. To access slides for this program, open the file *Types of Listening.ppt* on the accompanying CD. Copies of the slides for this training session are included at the end of chapter 9 (slides 9–11 through 9–20).

♦ PowerPoint presentation: The Listening Process. To access slides for this program, open the file *The Listening Process.ppt* on the accompanying CD. Copies of the slides for this training session are included at the end of chapter 9 (slides 9–21 through 9–38).

For the participants:

♦ Writing instruments/blank paper

Sample Agenda

8:00 a.m.   Content Module 10–1: Participant Introductions (chapter 10) (45 minutes; varies by class size)

            Objective: Prepare participants to help each other learn.

8:45   Content Module 10–2: Listening Defined (chapter 10) (1 hour)

            Objective: Understand what listening is, the importance of properly defining *listening*, and its behaviors.

9:45   Break (15 minutes)

10:00   Content Module 10–4: Types of Listening (chapter 10) (2 hours)

            Objective: Understand the primary types of listening and tips for using each of them to listen effectively.

12:00   Lunch (1 hour)

1:00   Begin Content Module 10–5: The Listening Process (chapter 10) (1 hour)

Objective: Understand a process to use for listening with specific steps for greater effectiveness.

2:00   Break (10 minutes)

2:10   Continue Content Module 10–5: The Listening Process (1 hour, 15 minutes)

3:25   Close (5 minutes)

Objective: Reinforce learning points.

3:30   Participants dismissed

Sample Agenda Two

This agenda is based on an identified need to improve the ability of learners to listen more effectively and to be aware of their particular behaviors when listening.

Time

- ♦ 8 hours, 20 minutes

Materials

For the instructor:

- ♦ Content Module 10–1: Participant Introductions

- ♦ Content Module 10–2: Listening Defined

- ♦ Content Module 10–3: Listening Self-Assessment

- ♦ Content Module 10–6: Nonverbal Communication

- ♦ Content Module 10–7: Effective Listening Behavior

- ♦ Content Module 10–8: The Bad Listener

- ♦ Structured Experience 12–1: Listening Buddies

- ♦ Structured Experience 12–6: Nonverbal Nonsense

- ♦ Structured Experience 12–7: Culture Shock

- ♦ Structured Experience 12–8: Fact or Fiction?

- ♦ Structured Experience 12–9: Driven to Distraction

- PowerPoint presentation: Listening Defined. To access slides for this program, open the file *Listening Defined.ppt* on the accompanying CD. Copies of the slides for this training session are included at the end of chapter 9 (slides 9–1 through 9–10).

- PowerPoint presentation: Nonverbal Communication. To access slides for this program, open the file *Nonverbal Communication.ppt* on the accompanying CD. Copies of the slides for this training session are included at the end of chapter 9 (slides 9–39 through 9–46).

- PowerPoint presentation: Effective Listening Behavior. To access slides for this program, open the file *Effective Listening Behavior.ppt* on the accompanying CD. Copies of the slides for this training session are included at the end of chapter 9 (slides 9–47 through 9–53).

- PowerPoint presentation: The Bad Listener. To access slides for this program, open the file *The Bad Listener.ppt* on the accompanying CD. Copies of the slides for this training session are included at the end of chapter 9 (slides 9–54 through 9–59).

For the participants:

- Assessment 11–2: Listening Self-Assessment

- Handout 12–1: Emotion Word Slips

- Handout 12–2: Cultural Differences in Nonverbal Communication

- Handout 12–3: Argument Analysis

- Writing instruments/blank paper

Sample Agenda

8:00 a.m.   Content Module 10–1: Participant Introductions (chapter 10) (45 minutes; varies by class size)

Objective: Prepare participants to help each other learn.

8:45   Content Module 10–2: Listening Defined (chapter 10) (1 hour)

Objective: Understand what listening is, the importance of properly defining *listening*, and its behaviors.

9:45   Break (15 minutes)

10:00   Content Module 10–3: Listening Self-Assessment (chapter 10) (1 hour)

Objective: Identify each participant's highest-impact learning.

11:00   Content Module 10–7: Effective Listening Behavior (chapter 10) (1 hour, 15 minutes)

Objective: Learn general principles and techniques for being an effective listener, including separating fact from generalization.

12:15   Lunch (1 hour)

1:15   Content Module 10–8: The Bad Listener (chapter 10) (1 hour)

Objective: Explore the many types of bad listening behaviors and how to recognize them.

2:15   Break (15 minutes)

2:30   Content Module 10–6: Nonverbal Communication (chapter 10) (1 hour, 45 minutes)

Objective: Understand the importance of nonverbal communication when listening.

4:15   Close (5 minutes)

Objective: Reinforce learning points.

4:20   Participants dismissed

Sample Agenda Three

This agenda is designed to strengthen the listening skills of the participants.

Time

♦ 8 hours, 15 minutes

Materials

For the instructor:

♦ Content Module 10–1: Participant Introductions

- Content Module 10–3: Listening Self-Assessment

- Content Module 10–9: Paraphrasing

- Content Module 10–10: Empathic Listening

- Content Module 10–11: Giving and Receiving Feedback

- Structured Experience 12–10: Paraphrasing Partners

- Structured Experience 12–11: Empathic Listening Practice

- Structured Experience 12–12: Fun With Feedback

- PowerPoint presentation: Paraphrasing. To access slides for this program, open the file *Paraphrasing.ppt* on the accompanying CD. Copies of the slides for this training session are included at the end of chapter 9 (slides 9–60 through 9–69).

- PowerPoint presentation: Empathic Listening. To access slides for this program, open the file *Empathic Listening.ppt* on the accompanying CD. Copies of the slides for this training session are included at the end of chapter 9 (slides 9–70 through 9–79).

- PowerPoint presentation: Giving and Receiving Feedback. To access slides for this program, open the file *Giving and Receiving Feedback.ppt* on the accompanying CD. Copies of the slides for this training session are included at the end of chapter 9 (slides 9–80 through 9–91).

For the participants:

- Assessment 11–2: Listening Self-Assessment

- Assessment 11–7: Feedback Self-Assessment

- Training Instrument 11–2: Empathic Listening Observation Checklist

- Training Instrument 11–3: Feedback Observation Worksheet

- Handout 12–4: Feedback Role-Play Scenarios

- Writing instruments

Sample Agenda

8:00 a.m.   Content Module 10–1: Participant Introductions (chapter 10) (45 minutes; varies by class size)

Objective: Prepare participants to help each other learn.

8:45	Content Module 10–3: Listening Self-Assessment (chapter 10) (1 hour)

Objective: Identify each participant's highest-impact learning.

9:45	Break (15 minutes)

10:00	Content Module 10–9: Paraphrasing (chapter 10) (1 hour, 30 minutes)

Objective: Understand the elements and techniques of paraphrasing, one of many helpful listening techniques.

11:30	Lunch (1 hour)

12:30	Content Module 10–10: Empathic Listening (chapter 10) (1 hour, 30 minutes)

Objective: Learn a common listening technique that is especially effective in diffusing emotionally charged situations or dealing with conflict.

2:00	Break (10 minutes)

2:10	Content Module 10–11: Giving and Receiving Feedback (chapter 10) (2 hours)

Objective: Learn principles and techniques for giving and receiving feedback effectively.

4:10	Close (5 Minutes)

Objective: Reinforce learning points.

4:15	Participants dismissed

Step-by-Step Planning

Just before the training session:

- Arrive early at the facility.

- Set up and test equipment (for example, laptop, projector, flipcharts).

- Confirm refreshments.

At the training session:

- Introduce yourself to the participants. Include a description of your role in the training process and your training and work experience. First impressions count, and this is your chance to establish credibility with the participants.

- If you do not use the participant introductions' exercise, ask the participants to introduce themselves by sharing their names, roles, and what they would like to gain from the training. Let them know they will be helping each other learn.

- Review the agenda and learning objectives with the participants.

- Go through the selected content modules.

- Ask for questions, and test for understanding frequently.

- Close the session with an opportunity for the participants to ask questions. If appropriate, offer your help and availability on an ongoing basis.

What to Do Next

- Identify the training participants. Assess their most critical training needs or identify the competencies the organization seeks to develop.

- Determine the agenda using the highest value content modules based on your needs assessment or the required competencies.

- Schedule the session.

- Arrange a facility for the training session.

- Invite participants. Check for any special dietary needs.

- Send a confirmation to participants. Include an agenda and any prework with the confirmation.

- Prepare training materials (handouts, overheads, presentations, and exercise materials).

- Order food and beverages.

◆

Multi-Day Session

- ◆ Advice on choosing the content for training sessions
- ◆ Step-by-step preparation and training delivery instructions
- ◆ Sample agendas

The materials in this book have been designed to meet a variety of training needs and timeframes. This chapter covers designs suitable for day-and-a-half and two-day training sessions.

As noted in chapter 8, longer learning experiences might raise concerns that participants will be overloaded with information. You can avoid this by designing programs that allow participants to learn efficiently and at their own pace. The purpose of this chapter is to present a significant amount of content in a multi-day session by mixing short, to-the-point theory and models with experiential exercises and assessments. This keeps the participants from feeling overwhelmed and, instead, produces an enjoyable, fruitful learning experience.

In addition, there are important benefits associated with extended learning experiences. Although a shorter program might be seen as part of a typical workday, a longer program can become a memorable life experience for the participant, especially if it is held at an off-site venue and includes an overnight stay. A multi-day design provides ample opportunity to create the learning environment (as discussed in chapter 4) and establish participants as learning partners. Discussion during breaks, meals, and evening activities often provides valuable feedback and learning. It often takes a different physical environment and a complete break from daily routine for participants to focus on learning.

Multi-day sessions are appropriate for group training. The learning environment is created and enriched by the backgrounds and experiences of a variety of participants. For multi-day sessions, groups of between 12 and 24 participants are most conducive to a learning environment. Smaller groups can limit the richness of group interactions, and larger groups can become unwieldy for the facilitator and can depersonalize the learning experience.

Please note that although illustrative designs are included, the trainer should adapt them to fit his or her specific purposes. Each design can be modified to take into account the available resources, the learning readiness of potential participants, and, above all, the assessed development needs of the target audience.

Objectives and Use

The objectives of a multi-day training session are to free participants from their daily routines so they can understand the learning content that is of greatest value, as well as build relationships between the trainer and the participants. The group setting and time available for interaction allow for rich and diverse discussion of the various topics.

Note: Residential programs held at appealing off-site facilities can also be used to create a special learning experience.

A multi-day training session is appropriate for the following circumstances:

- The targeted, available audience for training is 12 participants or more.

- The targeted audience requires comprehensive training in all areas of relevant content.

- Training facilities for groups are available.

- Participants are available for multiple days.

- Funding for meals and possibly an off-site location is available.

Choosing the Content

Any of the content modules in this book can be used for multi-day training sessions. Although a multi-day session allows time to cover all of the content modules, you may still need to perform a needs assessment of the participant group or review the competencies the organization seeks to develop. Include only those modules indicated by your needs assessment.

With a session that covers multiple days, you have to consider providing meals and possibly overnight accommodations. Hunger and thirst are enemies to the learning environment, so offer beverages and snacks at the breaks, as well as meals at appropriate times, so your participants' biological needs are met. Keep participants together during meals to encourage continued discussion of learning points. This also helps to strengthen the relationships among participants and, therefore, helps support the learning environment. Much discussion and feedback occurs during dinner after a long day of training. As noted in chapter 8, scheduled meals discourage participants from going back to the office and getting distracted from their learning focus. Moreover, providing meals helps to keep your session on schedule because participants are less likely to come back late from the lunch break.

All of the content modules in this book are included in one of the following sample agendas. The timing of the modules assumes that all of the structured experiences will be included.

The placement of the "Participant Introductions," "Listening Defined," and "Listening Self-Assessment" modules is important. They should be offered at the beginning of the session because they help focus the participants' learning by creating the context for the remaining content modules.

Sample Agenda, Day One

MATERIALS

For the instructor:

- ◆ Content Module 10–1: Participant Introductions

- ◆ Content Module 10–2: Listening Defined

- ◆ Content Module 10–3: Listening Self-Assessment

- ◆ Content Module 10–4: Types of Listening

- ◆ Content Module 10–5: The Listening Process

- ◆ Structured Experience 12–1: Listening Buddies

- ◆ Structured Experience 12–2: What's That Sound?

- ◆ Structured Experience 12–3: Newsworthy Note-Taking

- ◆ Structured Experience 12–4: Having a Ball

- Structured Experience 12–5: Memorize This

- Training Instrument 11–1: Memory Game Word Lists

- Newspaper article of medium length

- Tennis or other medium-sized rubber balls for small groups

- PowerPoint presentation: Listening Defined. To access slides for this program, open the file *Listening Defined.ppt* on the accompanying CD. Copies of the slides for this training session are included at the end of chapter 9 (slides 9–1 through 9–10).

- PowerPoint presentation: Types of Listening. To access slides for this program, open the file *Types of Listening.ppt* on the accompanying CD. Copies of the slides for this training session are included at the end of chapter 9 (slides 9–11 through 9–20).

- PowerPoint presentation: The Listening Process. To access slides for this program, open the file *The Listening Process.ppt* on the accompanying CD. Copies of the slides for this training session are included at the end of chapter 9 (slides 9–21 through 9–38).

For the participants:

- Assessment 11–2: Listening Self-Assessment

- Writing instruments/blank paper

Sample Agenda

8:00 a.m. Content Module 10–1: Participant Introductions (chapter 10) (45 minutes; varies by class size)

Objective: Prepare participants to help each other learn.

8:45 Content Module 10–2: Listening Defined (chapter 10) (1 hour)

Objective: Understand what listening is, the importance of properly defining *listening,* and its behaviors.

9:45 Break (15 minutes)

10:00 Content Module 10–3: Listening Self-Assessment (chapter 10) (1 hour)

Objective: Identify each participant's highest-impact learning.

11:00   Begin Content Module 10–4: Types of Listening (chapter 10) (1 hour)

                   Objective: Understand the primary types of listening and tips for using each of them to listen effectively.

12:00   Lunch (1 hour)

1:00   Continue Content Module 10–4: Types of Listening (1 hour)

2:00   Begin Content Module 10–5: The Listening Process (chapter 10) (1 hour)

                   Objective: Understand a process to use for listening with specific steps for greater effectiveness.

3:00   Break (15 minutes)

3:15   Continue Content Module 10–5: The Listening Process (1 hour, 15 minutes)

4:30   Close (5 minutes)

                   Objective: Reinforce learning points.

6:00   Dinner (if at an off-site location)

7:00   After-dinner activities (if at a residential off-site location)

Sample Agenda, Day Two (Full-Day Option)

MATERIALS

For the instructor:

- ◆ Content Module 10–6: Nonverbal Communication

- ◆ Content Module 10–7: Effective Listening Behaviors

- ◆ Content Module 10–8: The Bad Listener

- ◆ Content Module 10–9: Paraphrasing

- ◆ Content Module 10–10: Empathic Listening

- ◆ Structured Experience 12–6: Nonverbal Nonsense

- ◆ Structured Experience 12–7: Culture Shock

◆ Structured Experience 12–8: Fact or Fiction?

◆ Structured Experience 12–9: Driven to Distraction

◆ Structured Experience 12–10: Paraphrasing Partners

◆ Structured Experience 12–11: Empathic Listening Practice

◆ PowerPoint presentation: Nonverbal Communication. To access slides for this program, open the file *Nonverbal Communication.ppt* on the accompanying CD. Copies of the slides for this training session are included at the end of chapter 9 (slides 9–39 through 9–46).

◆ PowerPoint presentation: Effective Listening Behavior. To access slides for this program, open the file *Effective Listening Behavior.ppt* on the accompanying CD. Copies of the slides for this training session are included at the end of chapter 9 (slides 9–47 through 9–53).

◆ PowerPoint presentation: The Bad Listener. To access slides for this program, open the file *The Bad Listener.ppt* on the accompanying CD. Copies of the slides for this training session are included at the end of chapter 9 (slides 9–54 through 9–59).

◆ PowerPoint presentation: Paraphrasing. To access slides for this program, open the file *Paraphrasing.ppt* on the accompanying CD. Copies of the slides for this training session are included at the end of chapter 9 (slides 9–60 through 9–69).

◆ PowerPoint presentation: Empathic Listening. To access slides for this program, open the file *Empathic Listening.ppt* on the accompanying CD. Copies of the slides for this training session are included at the end of chapter 9 (slides 9–70 through 9–79).

For the participants:

◆ Handout 12–1: Emotion Word Slips

◆ Handout 12–2: Cultural Differences in Nonverbal Communication

◆ Handout 12–3: Argument Analysis

◆ Training Instrument 11–2: Empathic Listening Observation Checklist

◆ Writing instruments/blank paper

Sample Agenda

8:00 a.m.   Content Module 10–6: Nonverbal Communication (chapter 10) (1 hour, 45 minutes)

Objective: Understand the importance of nonverbal communication.

9:45   Break (15 minutes)

10:00   Content Module 10–7: Effective Listening Behavior (chapter 10) (1 hour, 15 minutes)

Objective: Learn general principles and techniques for being an effective listener, including separating fact from generalization.

11:15   Content Module 10–8: The Bad Listener (chapter 10) (1 hour)

Objective: Explore the many types of bad listening behaviors and how to recognize them.

12:15   Lunch (1 hour)

1:15   Content Module 10–9: Paraphrasing (chapter 10) (1 hour, 30 minutes)

Objective: Understand the elements and techniques of paraphrasing, one of many helpful listening techniques.

2:45   Break (15 minutes)

3:00   Content Module 10–10: Empathic Listening (chapter 10) (1 hour, 30 minutes)

Objective: Learn a common listening technique that is especially effective in diffusing emotionally charged situations or dealing with conflict.

4:30   Close (5 minutes)

Objective: Reinforce learning points.

Sample Agenda, Day Two (Half-Day Option)

MATERIALS

For the instructor:

◆ Content Module 10–10: Empathic Listening

- Content Module 10–11: Giving and Receiving Feedback

- Structured Experience 12–11: Empathic Listening Practice

- Structured Experience 12–12: Fun With Feedback

- PowerPoint presentation: Empathic Listening. To access slides for this program, open the file *Empathic Listening.ppt* on the accompanying CD. Copies of the slides for this training session are included at the end of chapter 9 (slides 9–70 through 9–79).

- PowerPoint presentation: Giving and Receiving Feedback. To access slides for this program, open the file *Giving and Receiving Feedback.ppt* on the accompanying CD. Copies of the slides for this training session are included at the end of chapter 9 (slides 9–80 through 9–91).

For the participants:

- Assessment 11-7: Feedback Self-Assessment

- Training Instrument 11–2: Empathic Listening Observation Checklist

- Training Instrument 11–3: Feedback Observation Worksheet

- Handout 12–4: Feedback Role-Play Scenarios

- Writing instruments

Sample Agenda

8:00 a.m.   Content Module 10–10: Empathic Listening (chapter 10) (1 hour, 30 minutes)

Objective: Learn a common listening technique that is especially effective in diffusing emotionally charged situations or dealing with conflict.

9:30   Break (15 minutes)

9:45   Content Module 10–11: Giving and Receiving Feedback (chapter 10) (2 hours)

Objective: Learn principles and techniques for giving and receiving feedback effectively.

11:45   Close (5 Minutes)

Objective: Reinforce learning points.

Step-by-Step Planning

Just before the training session:

- ◆ If this is a residential program, confirm rooming list with hotel.

- ◆ Arrive early at the facility.

- ◆ Set up and test equipment (for example, laptop, projector, flip-charts).

- ◆ Confirm refreshments.

At the training session:

- ◆ Introduce yourself to the participants. Include a description of your role in the training process and your training and work experience. First impressions count, and this is your chance to establish credibility with the participants.

- ◆ If you do not use the participant introduction exercise, ask the participants to introduce themselves by sharing their names, roles, and what they would like to gain from the training. Let them know they will be helping each other learn.

- ◆ Review each day's agenda and learning objectives with the participants.

- ◆ Go through the selected content modules.

- ◆ Ask for questions, and test for understanding frequently.

- ◆ Close each day with an opportunity for the participants to ask questions.

What to Do Next

- ◆ Identify the training participants. Assess their most critical training needs or identify the competencies the organization seeks to develop.

- ◆ Design the agenda using the highest value content modules based on your needs assessment or the required competencies.

- ◆ Schedule the session.

- ◆ Arrange a facility for the training session. Book a block of rooms if this is a residential program.

◆ Invite participants. Check for any special dietary needs. If this is a residential program, check for rooming requirements (smoking/ nonsmoking, single/double bed, and so forth).

◆ Send a confirmation to participants. Include an agenda and any prework with the confirmation.

◆ Prepare training materials (handouts, overheads, presentations, and exercise materials).

◆ Order food and beverages.

Slide 9–1

Listening Defined

Lisa J. Downs

American Society for Training and Development

Slide 9–2

To Listen Is To...

- Hear something with thoughtful attention; give consideration
- Make an effort to hear something
- Give heed to; pay attention

Slide 9–3

Listening Is Not...

- The act of hearing
- Preparing a response
- Anticipating what the speaker will say
- Ignoring the speaker

Slide 9–4

Why Listen?

- Builds deeper relationships
- Creates new ways to approach issues
- Leads to trust
- Clarifies information
- Diffuses emotional situations
- Develops additional insight

Slide 9–5

Listen Carefully When...

- Diffusing emotionally charged situations
- Giving and receiving feedback
- Asking and answering questions
- Discussing ideas and strategy
- Receiving others' opinions
- Problem-solving

Slide 9–6

Did You Know?

The average adult has an attention span of only 7 minutes

What are the implications of this for listening?

Slide 9–7

Why Don't We Listen?

- In a hurry
- Distracted
- Out of practice
- Follow stereotypes
- Not interested
- Exhausted

Slide 9–8

Basic Steps to Listening

- Hearing
- Attending
- Understanding
- Responding
- Remembering

Slide 9–9

Keep in Mind...

- Listening in an active, not a passive activity
- When done effectively, listening should make you feel tired when the speaker is finished

Slide 9–10

Consider...

"Listening well is as powerful a means of communication and influence as to talk well."

- John Marshall

How do you interpret this idea?

Slide 9–11

Types of Listening

Lisa J. Downs

American Society for Training and Development

Slide 9–12

Four Primary Types

- Informational
- Critical
- Appreciative
- Empathic

Slide 9–13

Informational Listening

- Goal is to accurately receive information from another person

- Does not involve criticizing or judging, only learning

- Sample scenarios include following directions, exchanging ideas, or learning about someone through personal stories

Slide 9–14

Tips for Informational Listening

- Focus on key points
- Take notes
- Link common ideas together
- Repeat information silently or aloud

Slide 9–15

Critical Listening

- Goal is to consider ideas heard from a speaker to decide if they make sense

- Helps with making decisions based on logic and evidence, rather than on emotion

- Sample scenarios include listening to a political debate, a talk radio program, or a restaurant critique

Slide 9–16

Tips for Critical Listening

- Look for evidence to support ideas
- Consider the source of the evidence
- Check for logical reasoning
- Make a special effort to understand what the speaker is saying

Slide 9–17

Appreciative Listening

- Goal is to listen for enjoyment or entertainment

- Does not involve analyzing or evaluating information

- Sample scenarios include attending a rock concert, listening to music at home, or going to a Broadway show

Slide 9–18

Tips for Appreciative Listening

- Make an effort to block out background noise

- Avoid engaging in conversation

- Turn off electronic devices (cell phones, PDAs, watch alarms, etc.)

Slide 9–19

Empathic Listening

- Goal is to understand what the speaker is saying and feeling

- Involves making an effort to look at the world through someone else's view

- Sample scenarios include listening to an irate client, helping a friend with an emotional situation, or listening to someone who received bad news

Slide 9–20

Tips for Empathic Listening

- Paraphrase what the other person says to seek understanding

- Focus on the speaker's emotions

- Avoid judging or criticizing; let the person "vent" if needed

Slide 9–21

The Listening Process

Lisa J. Downs

American Society of Training and Development

Slide 9–22

Needs Fulfilled by Listening

- To release feelings or "vent"

- To have emotional intimacy

- To be validated and boost self-esteem

Slide 9–23

Step 1: Hearing

- Hearing occurs when sound waves strike the ear

- Sound is transferred along neural pathways to parts of the brain

- Hearing is a prerequisite to listening

- Temporary hearing loss may occur with exposure to the same loudness or tone

Slide 9–24

Hearing Techniques

- Be in close proximity to the speaker

- Minimize distractions if possible

- Move to a quiet location if needed

- Focus on what the speaker is saying

Slide 9–25

Common Distractions

External:

- Other people's noise
- Television
- Stereo or radio
- Alarms or loud noises
- Telephone
- Speaker's mannerisms or volume

Slide 9–26

Common Distractions

Internal:

- Emotions toward speaker
- Prejudice or bias
- Lack of interest
- Stress
- Conflicting priorities
- Negative attitude

Slide 9–27

Step 2: Attending

- Attending involves filtering out some messages and focusing on others
- Attending is a psychological choice
- Some sounds are brought to the foreground while others stay in the background
- People may attend more when there is a benefit for doing so

Slide 9–28

Attending Techniques

- Get ready to listen by being ready, both mentally and physically
- Adjust to the listening goal of the scenario; intensity will vary
- Avoid rehearsing responses and watch interrupting

Slide 9–29

Step 3: Understanding

- Understanding refers to making sense of a message by assigning meaning to it
- Vocabulary affects understanding
- It's possible to hear and attend to a message without understanding
- Interpretation of a message leads to evaluating its importance

Slide 9–30

Understanding Techniques

- Ask if unsure about the meaning of a word or phrase
- Watch nonverbal cues to gauge tone and mood
- Focus on the purpose of a complex message

Slide 9–31

Step 4: Responding

- Responding consists of providing feedback to the speaker
- Feedback may be verbal and nonverbal
- Responding demonstrates active rather than passive behavior
- Responses must be appropriate to the situation

Slide 9–32

Responding Techniques

- Practice letting the speaker complete all thoughts
- Match the response to the goal of the listening
- Ask questions if needed to gain clarity

Slide 9–33

Types of Responses

- Verbal acknowledgment ("oh," "I see," "mm-hmm," etc.)
- Nonverbal (nodding head, leaning forward, smiling)
- Paraphrasing: putting into words another person's statement
- Questioning for clarification

Slide 9–34

Poor Responses

- Interrupting: breaking in before the speaker has a chance to finish a statement or thought
- Ignoring: not paying attention to the speaker or providing an irrelevant response

Slide 9–35

Poor Responses

- Deflecting: changing the subject, intentionally or unintentionally, to shift emphasis away from speaker
- Conflicting: exhibiting nonverbal behaviors in conflict with the verbal response (e.g., shaking head while agreeing to something)

Slide 9–36

Step 5: Remembering

- Remembering is the process of recalling information from memory
- People may forget immediately as much as half of what they hear
- General impressions of people and situations may be retained more often, especially if feelings are present
- Remembering is important in building relationships

Slide 9–37

Remembering Techniques

- Take notes
- Use a mnemonic device (memory aid) to help with recall
- Group similar ideas together
- Repeat names and keywords

Slide 9–38

Mnemonic Devices

- Acronyms: take first letters of items and form a word
- Word association: think of "trigger" words or rhymes to connect to items
- Chronological order: assign dates or sequences to items

Slide 9–39

Nonverbal Communication

Lisa J. Downs

American Society of Learning and Development

Slide 9–40

Nonverbals and Listening

- One of the most important aspects to effective listening is good nonverbal communication
- Research shows that as little as 7 to 30% of meaning of communication comes from words; the rest comes from body language

Slide 9–41

Nonverbals and Listening

- Effective listeners hear more than a speaker's words; they hear the emotional tone of voice as well
- Nonverbal aspect is mostly unconscious
- Nonverbal communication is the primary way to express emotion

Slide 9–42

Categories of Nonverbals

- Posture: can indicate tension, relaxation, or interest
- Body Orientation: can face toward or away from someone with head, feet, and body

Slide 9–43

Categories of Nonverbals

- Gestures: can convey certain messages or emphasize points
- Facial Expressions: can change quickly and show a variety of emotions

Slide 9–44

Categories of Nonverbals

- Eye Contact: can convey interest, attitude, dominance, or excitement
- Voice: can vary in tone, pitch, volume, and rate to get across different meanings and emotions

Slide 9–45

Nonverbal Listening Tips

- Establish eye contact with the speaker early in the conversation
- Lean forward to show interest
- Limit distracting mannerisms

Slide 9–46

Nonverbal Listening Tips

- Match facial expression to the situation
- Face the speaker with an open body posture
- Use appropriate vocal tone

Slide 9–47

Effective Listening Behavior

Lisa J. Downs

American Society of Training and Development

Slide 9–48

Is Anyone Listening?

- People spend more time each day listening than in any other activity
- People speak at 100-175 words per minute, but can listen intelligently at 600-800 words per minute

What are the implications of this data?

Slide 9–49

Techniques for Better Listening

- Listeners need to understand their own communication style (strengths and weaknesses)
- Nonverbal communication should be used frequently to provide feedback to the speaker

Slide 9–50

Techniques for Better Listening

- Be an active listener by listening with a purpose to avoid mind drift
- Practice listening skills with a trusted friend or family member
- Provide verbal feedback as appropriate

Slide 9–51

Techniques for Better Listening

- Go into conversations with an open mind
- Fully concentrate on the speaker's words and nonverbal cues
- Separate fact from generalization

Slide 9–52

Techniques for Better Listening

- Keep emotions in check to remain objective
- Take the orientation of "other" instead of "I"
- Focus only on sound in the foreground

Slide 9–53

Techniques for Better Listening

- Adopt a caring attitude
- Determine what information you need to know
- Be fully present "in the moment"

Slide 9–54

The Bad Listener

Lisa J. Downs

American Society for Training and Development

Slide 9–55

Types of Bad Listening

- Pseudolistening: giving the appearance of being a good listener while using a façade to mask real thoughts
- Stage-Hogging: consistently turning the topic of conversation away from the speaker and onto oneself

Slide 9–56

Types of Bad Listening

- Ambushing: listening carefully, but gathering information to use against the speaker at a later time
- Selective Listening: responding only to the parts of the conversation that interest the listener while tuning out everything else

Slide 9–57

Types of Bad Listening

- Defensive Listening: taking everything that is said as a personal attack
- Avoidant Listening: forgetting what is said if the subject is negative or something the listener would not like to manage

Slide 9–58

Bad Listening Behaviors

- Judging: letting negative views influence extent of paying attention
- Rehearsing: spending the bulk of the conversation preparing a response
- Problem-Solving: jumping into giving advice as soon as possible

Slide 9–59

Bad Listening Behaviors

- Debating: arguing with the listener regardless of what is said
- Daydreaming: thinking about topics unrelated to the conversation
- Agreeing: half-listening to satisfy the speaker but not being involved

Slide 9–60

Paraphrasing

Lisa J. Downs
American Society for Training and Development

Slide 9–61

Paraphrasing Defined

- Paraphrasing is an effective form of verbal feedback to use when listening

- It is not simply repetition or "parroting," but restating another person's statement in your own words to gain understanding

Slide 9–62

Paraphrasing Defined

- Paraphrasing enables the listener to clarify the speaker's meaning

- It also conveys interest in what the speaker is saying and helps create a supportive environment for the conversation

Slide 9–63

When to Paraphrase

- The listener is not completely sure he or she has fully understood the speaker's meaning

- The speaker is emotional and may be using highly charged language

- The listener needs better understanding of the message to respond well

Slide 9–64

When to Paraphrase

- The listener may react strongly to the message which can interfere with interpretation of the meaning

- The speaker may have a thick accent or is speaking a language that is not his/her primary one, possibly causing difficulty for the listener

Slide 9–65

Paraphrasing Example

Speaker: "I'm having a hard time communicating with Bill and I don't know what's going on."

Paraphrase: "It sounds like you're frustrated that you and Bill aren't getting along these days."

Speaker: "Yeah, and I'm just not sure what to do about it."

Slide 9–66

Paraphrasing Example

Speaker: "I thought I did a good job on that report I turned in, but I got it back from my boss today with corrections all over it."

Paraphrase: "If I'm hearing you correctly, seeing those corrections was a big surprise."

Speaker: "It threw me for a loop, that's for sure."

Slide 9–67

Paraphrasing Example

Speaker: "I feel awful today."

Paraphrase: "It sounds like you're coming down with a cold."

Speaker: "Actually, I'm just dreading having to present at the department meeting this afternoon."

Slide 9–68

Steps for Paraphrasing

1. Listen carefully to the speaker's message

2. Determine the meaning of the message

3. If you think a paraphrase is needed, restate the message in your own words to share the meaning you received

Slide 9–69

Paraphrasing Tips

- If the paraphrase is off target, the speaker will set the listener straight

- Paraphrasing may not be appropriate in all circumstances, especially for simple, quick verbal exchanges

- It may seem awkward at first, but it will become more natural with practice

Slide 9–70

Empathic Listening

Lisa J. Downs
American Society for Training and Development

Slide 9–71

Empathic Listening Defined

- Listening empathically means to listen with the intent to understand how the speaker *feels* in addition to understanding his or her ideas

- Showing empathy involves identifying with a person's emotions and situation, even if not in agreement with them

Slide 9–72

Empathic Listening Defined

- Empathic listening is typically an effective technique to use in emotional situations, when there is a problem that needs resolving, or if there is conflict present

- The goal is to enable the listener to share emotions free from judgment or criticism

Slide 9–73

Empathic Listening Formula

Acknowledge Speaker	Reflect Feelings	Describe Facts/Situation
↓	↓	↓
"You got...	upset...	when you didn't get promoted at work."

Adapted from: Burley-Allen, Madelyn. Listening: The Forgotten Skill (2nd edition). New York, NY: John Wiley & Sons, Inc., 1995.

Slide 9–74

Empathic Listening Formula

Phrases to help get started:

"You feel..."

"It seems like..."

"As I understand it, you sound..."

"It appears as if..."

"If I hear you correctly, you'd like..."

Slide 9–75

Empathic Listening Example

Speaker: "I can't believe what poor shape our finances are in. I think Karen is really mismanaging the budget and I'm worried."

Listener: "If I hear you correctly, you feel distressed about what's happening with the company's money."

Slide 9–76

Steps for Empathic Listening

1. Listen carefully to the speaker's messages, both verbal and nonverbal

2. Display an open, caring posture

3. Consider the speaker's emotional state

4. Calmly reflect back what you perceive the speaker's feelings and meaning to be

Slide 9–77

Behaviors to Avoid

- Questioning or Probing
- Judging
- Criticizing
- Lecturing
- Advising
- Interrupting
- Giving autobiographical responses (e.g. "when I was on that team...")

Slide 9–78

Empathic Listening Tips

- Be interested in the speaker
- Have good eye contact and body language
- Minimize distractions
- Invite the speaker to expand on his or her thoughts
- Respond in a tone that is appropriate for the situation

Slide 9–79

Points to Remember

- Empathic listening is about the speaker, not the listener

- It is not necessary to use empathic listening during an entire conversation; it is primarily a way to understand another person's point of view

Slide 9–80

Giving and Receiving Feedback

Lisa J. Downs

American Society for Training and Development

Slide 9–81

Feedback Defined

- Feedback is the response by a listener to a speaker's message

- It can be verbal or nonverbal, positive or constructive

- Giving and receiving feedback effectively is key for good listening

Slide 9–82

Feedback Defined

Effective Feedback Is...
- Timely
- Specific
- Descriptive
- Relevant
- Helpful
- Realistic

Slide 9–83

Steps for Giving Feedback

1. Ask the person if he or she is open to receiving feedback

2. Describe the person's behavior as specifically and accurately as possible, focusing on observations

3. Keep the tone of voice positive

Slide 9–84

Steps for Giving Feedback

4. Describe the impact of the person's behavior

5. Work with the person to identify alternate behaviors

6. Follow up with the person after an agreed-upon timeframe

Slide 9–85

Tips for Giving Feedback

- Be aware of your own reactions and feelings; question assumptions

- Avoid rushing to judgment or blame; keep an open mind

- Use paraphrasing and empathic listening techniques

Slide 9–86

Tips for Giving Feedback

- Consider the person's recent behavior

- Help the person explore ideas and action steps

- Be mindful of timing and location for the feedback conversation

Slide 9–87

Feedback Example

Speaker: "Jim, I've noticed something with your behavior in our team meetings. Would now be a good time to share my observation with you?"

Listener: "Sure, Kim. I'm at a stopping point in my work right now."

Speaker: "Great; thank you. When you don't seem to have project updates to share in our meetings, I feel concerned. Can you help me understand what's happening?"

Slide 9–88

Steps for Receiving Feedback

1. Ask for feedback to avoid any surprises

2. Consider any feedback as being in your best interest

3. Concentrate on listening to the other person

Slide 9–89

Steps for Receiving Feedback

4. Paraphrase what you hear to gain understanding

5. Ask clarifying questions if needed

6. Thank the person for taking an interest and tell him or her how you will use the feedback

Slide 9–90

Tips for Receiving Feedback

- Avoid becoming defensive; stay focused on the positive

- Ask for examples or specific observations if you do not hear any

- Do not ramble; listen more than speak

Slide 9–91

Tips for Receiving Feedback

- Do not interrupt the speaker

- Ask for feedback only when you want an honest response

- Follow through on commitments made during the conversation and update the person on progress

◆

Content Modules

- ◆ Detailed instructions for using the content modules

- ◆ Content modules 10–1 through 10–11

This chapter contains all of the content modules referenced in the sample agendas in previous chapters. The term *content* refers to the emphases within the modules. Each content module is a self-contained learning experience that can be used either as a stand-alone training session or incorporated into a broader agenda. The interactive designs explore content areas in a step-by-step fashion. They are handy, readily available resources to help facilitators address the issues that learners face in effective listening training.

Using the Content Modules

These content modules are the building blocks of a training program for coaches. Each module includes, as appropriate:

- ◆ Step-by-step instructions

- ◆ Key learning points

- ◆ Discussion questions

- ◆ A list of materials to be used in each module, including

  - ◆ Training instruments

- PowerPoint presentations

- Structured exercises

Trainers should review the content module, along with all of the resources used in the module. After becoming familiar with the content, follow the step-by-step instructions for facilitating the module. Time estimates are provided for each module and each step, but the time needed for activities may vary, depending on the facilitators and the participants.

A trainer can modify these modules to comply with the organization's priorities; the readiness level of potential participants; or the resources in terms of time, space, and availability of trainees. These modules apply many of the principles of adult learning specified in chapter 3 of this book. It is important that the trainer understands and is committed to these principles before undertaking revisions of the step-by-step approaches included here.

The Modules

The modules included in this chapter emphasize learning through participation, using the materials in this book. As recommended in chapter 2, it's important to conduct a needs assessment before deciding which modules will be used, how they will be modified, and how you will combine various modules into longer sessions.

This section includes 11 modules:

- **Content Module 10–1: Participant Introductions.** This module helps create a collaborative learning environment; it introduces participants to each other and suggests that each person's role is to contribute to the learning process.

- **Content Module 10–2: Listening Defined.** The term *listening* can mean different things to different people. This module addresses the importance of properly defining this term and specifies the behaviors that are involved in listening.

- **Content Module 10–3: Listening Self-Assessment.** This module uses a self-assessment instrument (Assessment 11–2) to help participants identify areas in which their learning can have the most impact. It also provides an action plan so that learners can identify steps they can take to improve their listening skills.

- **Content Module 10–4: Types of Listening.** In this module, participants learn about the four primary types of listening, and they receive tips for using each of them. They also have the opportunity to practice two of these types of listening in the learning environment.

- **Content Module 10–5: The Listening Process.** This module outlines a five-step process for effective listening. It includes common distractions when listening, as well as techniques for each of the steps.

- **Content Module 10–6: Nonverbal Communication.** This module examines the important role that nonverbal communication plays in listening. It includes discussion of the different categories of nonverbals and tips for effective nonverbal communication.

- **Content Module 10–7: Effective Listening Behavior.** This module includes general principles and techniques for being an effective listener, and it teaches participants to be able to separate fact from generalization, an important aspect of good listening.

- **Content Module 10–8: The Bad Listener.** This module explores the many types of bad listening behaviors and how to recognize them. Participants also get firsthand experience in dealing with some bad listeners and strategies to remedy this problem.

- **Content Module 10–9: Paraphrasing.** One of the many listening strategies, paraphrasing is an effective technique that produces good results for many people. This module introduces the strategy and provides steps and tips for successful paraphrasing.

- **Content Module 10–10: Empathic Listening.** A primary type of listening, empathic listening is a common technique that is effective in diffusing emotionally charged situations or dealing with conflict. This module includes a formula to follow for empathic listening, as well as the opportunity for participants to practice the technique.

- **Content Module 10–11: Giving and Receiving Feedback.** This module outlines the principles and techniques for giving and receiving feedback effectively. It also includes an assessment so learners can identify areas in which they may need to improve their behavior, since listening is a primary component in the feedback process.

Content Module 10–1: Participant Introductions

This module helps create a collaborative learning environment. It introduces participants to each other and suggests that each person's role is to contribute to the learning process.

TIME

- ◆ 10 minutes, and an additional 3 minutes for each participant

AGENDA

- ◆ Discuss key points. (5 minutes)
- ◆ Facilitate introduction exercise. (approximately 3 minutes per participant)
- ◆ Review some of the strengths and learning priorities of participants. (5 minutes)

KEY POINTS

- ◆ Everyone has strengths in listening and communicating, and each person can contribute to learning.
- ◆ One person's development needs are often another's strengths.

INTRODUCTION EXERCISE

Use a variety of introduction techniques based on the time available and the facilitator's preference. One good technique is to ask participants to share information about themselves with the other participants, identifying what they each have in common. At the end of each person's introduction, ask for a show of hands from participants who had at least one thing in common with another person regarding his or her listening skills. Then, from this group, ask for a volunteer or two to share their common items. Introductions should include this information:

- ◆ Name
- ◆ Area or function in which the participant works
- ◆ How long the participant has been in that role or with the same organization
- ◆ One thing the participant does well when it comes to listening
- ◆ One thing the participant would like to learn about being a more effective listener

Content Module 10–2: Listening Defined

The term *listening* can mean different things to different people. This module addresses the importance of properly defining this term and specifies the behaviors that are involved in listening.

TIME

- ◆ 1 hour

MATERIALS

- ◆ Structured Experience 12–1: Listening Buddies (chapter 12)

- ◆ PowerPoint presentation *Listening Defined.ppt* (on the CD)

AGENDA

- ◆ Lead group through the first discussion question below. (5 minutes)

- ◆ Review PowerPoint presentation "Listening Defined." (25 minutes)

Discussion questions 2 and 3 are included in the presentation.

- ◆ Facilitate Structured Experience 12–1: Listening Buddies. (30 minutes)

KEY POINTS

- ◆ Listening means to hear something with thoughtful attention; we must make an effort to hear something and give heed to it.

- ◆ Listening is not simply hearing sound or preparing what we will say in response to a speaker.

- ◆ There are many different reasons to listen, including building better relationships, clarifying information, diffusing emotional situations, and developing trust.

- ◆ Listening is an active activity, not a passive one. To listen well, we need to put a lot of energy into the process and eliminate factors that may interfere.

DISCUSSION QUESTIONS

1. What does listening mean to you?

2. The average adult has an attention span of only seven minutes. What are the implications of this for listening?

3. Listening well is as powerful and influential as talking well. How do you interpret this idea?

Content Module 10–3: Listening Self-Assessment

This module uses a self-assessment instrument (Assessment 11–2) to help participants identify areas in which their learning can have the most impact. It also provides an action plan so that learners can identify steps they can take to improve their listening skills.

TIME

♦ 1 hour

MATERIALS

♦ Assessment 11–2: Listening Self-Assessment (chapter 11)

AGENDA

♦ Discuss key points. (5 minutes)

♦ Administer the assessment and have participants review the section called "Why These Behaviors Are Important." (15 minutes)

♦ Ask participants to divide into pairs and help each other complete the "Plan for Self-Improvement" at the end of the assessment. (20 minutes)

♦ Lead entire group through discussion questions. (20 minutes)

KEY POINTS

♦ Effective listeners have clearly defined behaviors and are able to focus on the speaker, filter information, and provide feedback.

♦ It's important to identify which listening behaviors are important to you in your interactions with others and to practice these behaviors.

♦ Knowing your listening strengths and weaknesses will help you be a better listener.

DISCUSSION QUESTIONS

1. How can the strengths you identified in the self-assessment help you be an effective listener? (Ask for examples from past experiences.)

2. What can you do specifically to improve the areas identified in your self-assessment?

Content Module 10–4: Types of Listening

In this module, participants learn about the four primary types of listening, and they receive tips for using each of them. They also have the opportunity to practice two of these types of listening in the learning environment.

TIME

- ◆ 2 hours

MATERIALS

- ◆ Structured Experience 12–2: What's That Sound? (chapter 12)

- ◆ Structured Experience 12–3: Newsworthy Note-Taking (chapter 12)

- ◆ PowerPoint presentation *Types of Listening.ppt* (on the CD)

AGENDA

- ◆ Lead group through Discussion Question 1. (5 minutes)

- ◆ Facilitate Structured Experience 12–2: What's That Sound? (30 minutes)

- ◆ Review PowerPoint presentation "Types of Listening." (25 minutes)

- ◆ Point out to the participants that what they did in Structured Experience 12–2 was an example of appreciative listening and that they soon will practice informative listening.

- ◆ Discuss the key points. Lead participants through the remaining discussion questions. (15 minutes)

- ◆ Facilitate Structured Experience 12–3: Newsworthy Note-Taking. (45 minutes)

KEY POINTS

- ◆ The four primary types of listening are informational, critical, appreciative, and empathic, and each has its own characteristics and strategies.

- ◆ Critical listening involves using logic and facts to make a decision. Evidence is a key component of this type of listening.

♦ Empathic listening emphasizes understanding someone else's feelings, even if you disagree. This type of listening may take a lot of practice to use (and is expanded upon in Content Module 10–10).

♦ Listeners should decide which type of listening to use based on the situation. In many cases, the best choice is clear; however, it is not uncommon for a seemingly informational listening scenario to become an empathic listening situation.

 ## DISCUSSION QUESTIONS

1. Think of your most common listening situations. Do you listen more for content, or are you more often a sounding board? Why do you think that is?

2. What types of appreciative listening do you enjoy? What do you gain from these experiences?

3. What's an example of being in a critical listening situation? How did you make your decision?

4. Are you comfortable with silence? Is having background noise a comfort to you? Why or why not?

Content Module 10–5: The Listening Process

A five-step process for effective listening is covered in this module. Common distractions when listening are discussed, as well as techniques for each of the steps.

TIME

- ◆ 2 hours, 15 minutes

MATERIALS

- ◆ Training Instrument 11–1: Memory Game Word Lists (chapter 11)

- ◆ Structured Experience 12–4: Having a Ball (chapter 12)

- ◆ Structured Experience 12–5: Memorize This (chapter 12)

- ◆ PowerPoint presentation *The Listening Process.ppt* (on the CD)

AGENDA

- ◆ Lead group through Discussion Question 1. (5 minutes)

- ◆ Review slides 1–10 in PowerPoint presentation "The Listening Process." (20 minutes)

- ◆ Facilitate Structured Experience 12–4: Having a Ball. (60 minutes)

- ◆ Review remaining slides in PowerPoint presentation "The Listening Process." (10 minutes)

- ◆ Discuss the key points. Lead participants through Discussion Questions 2 and 3. (10 minutes)

- ◆ Facilitate Structured Experience 12–5: Memorize This. (30 minutes)

KEY POINTS

- ◆ Listening is a five-step process that includes everything from hearing to understanding and remembering the messages that you hear.

- ◆ A variety of external and internal distractions can surface when listening, and it is up to the listener to make a conscious effort to minimize these distractions as much as possible.

♦ We can prepare ourselves to listen physically and mentally, and we can adapt to listening situations quickly to better understand and respond appropriately to a speaker's message.

♦ A number of poor responses as a listener include interrupting or ignoring the speaker and changing the subject or giving conflicting nonverbal messages.

DISCUSSION QUESTIONS

1. What needs do you think can be fulfilled when others really listen to us?

2. Why is it important to have a process for listening?

3. What are some techniques that haven't already been discussed that you use to help you recall information?

Content Module 10–6: Nonverbal Communication

This module looks at the important role that nonverbal communication plays in listening. It includes discussion of the different categories of nonverbals, as well as tips for effective nonverbal communication.

TIME

- 1 hour, 40 minutes to 2 hours

MATERIALS

- Handout 12–1: Emotion Word Slips (chapter 12)

- Handout 12–2: Cultural Differences in Nonverbal Communication (chapter 12)

- Structured Experience 12–6: Nonverbal Nonsense (chapter 12)

- Structured Experience 12–7: Culture Shock (chapter 12)

- PowerPoint presentation *Nonverbal Communication.ppt* (on the CD)

AGENDA

- Facilitate Structured Experience 12–6: Nonverbal Nonsense. (35–45 minutes)

- Review PowerPoint presentation "Nonverbal Communication." (15–20 minutes)

- Facilitate Structured Experience 12–7: Culture Shock. (40 minutes)

- Discuss the key points. Lead the participants through the discussion questions. (10–15 minutes)

KEY POINTS

- Most of the meaning during communication is reflected in body language rather than in words.

♦ The many types of nonverbal communication to attend to when listening include gestures, tone of voice, posture, and facial expression.

♦ To be effective, establish eye contact with the speaker when listening to indicate focus and interest.

♦ It is important to match your nonverbal communication to the tone of the speaker and the conversation at hand.

DISCUSSION QUESTIONS

1. Was there a situation in which you received mixed messages from someone's nonverbal communication? What was the outcome?

2. What are some of your common mannerisms or nonverbals? Are there any you would eliminate or change when listening? Why or why not?

3. What are some techniques we can use to remind ourselves to pay attention to a speaker's nonverbal communication?

Content Module 10–7: Effective Listening Behavior

General principles and techniques for being an effective listener are covered in this module. It also includes separating fact from generalization, an important aspect of good listening.

TIME

- 1 hour, 15 minutes

MATERIALS

- Handout 12–3: Argument Analysis (chapter 12)

- Structured Experience 12–8: Fact or Fiction? (chapter 12)

- PowerPoint presentation *Effective Listening Behavior.ppt* (on the CD)

AGENDA

- Lead group through the first discussion question below. (5 minutes)

- Review PowerPoint presentation "Effective Listening Behavior." (15 minutes)

Discussion Question 2 is included in the presentation.

- Facilitate Structured Experience 12–8: Fact or Fiction? (45 minutes)

- Discuss key points. Lead the group through the remaining discussion questions. (10 minutes)

KEY POINTS

- We spend more time each day listening than doing any other activity, whether or not we consciously realize it.

- It is important to recognize your own communication style to use your strengths and mitigate weaknesses when listening.

- It's a good idea to practice listening skills with family and friends to improve in a safe environment.

◆ We should adopt a caring attitude when listening and keep our emotions in check so they do not interfere with the speaker's message.

◆ It is critical to separate fact from inference as a listener to be able to provide an appropriate response and maintain objectivity.

DISCUSSION QUESTIONS

1. Think about someone you know who you consider to be a good listener. What behavior does he or she exhibit that works well?

2. People speak at 100–175 words per minute, but can listen intelligently at 600–800 words per minute. What are the implications of this data on listening? (Some responses may be that this can lead to our minds drifting, that we may then formulate responses while listening, or that we may try to finish a speaker's sentences. This is all the more reason that we need to concentrate on listening.)

3. Was there an occasion in which you did not go into a conversation with an open mind? What happened?

4. What are some specific benefits to being nonjudgmental when listening?

Content Module 10–8: The Bad Listener

This module explores the many types of bad listening behaviors and how to recognize them. Participants also get firsthand experience in dealing with some bad listeners and strategies that will remedy the situation.

TIME

- 1 hour

MATERIALS

- Structured Experience 12–9: Driven to Distraction (chapter 12)

- PowerPoint presentation *The Bad Listener.ppt* (on the CD)

AGENDA

- Facilitate Structured Experience 12–9: Driven to Distraction. (40 minutes)

- Review PowerPoint presentation "The Bad Listener." (10 minutes)

- Discuss the key points. Lead the participants through the discussion questions. (10 minutes)

KEY POINTS

- Many forms of bad listening behavior exist, and we are probably all guilty of engaging in some of them.

- Pseudo-listening and selective listening are two common types of bad listening.

- Rehearsing, problem solving, and daydreaming are bad listening behaviors that many people engage in, often without being aware of it.

- To improve our listening skills, we must consciously be aware of our bad behaviors and take steps to correct them.

DISCUSSION QUESTIONS

1. Think about someone you know who you consider to be a poor listener. What behaviors does he or she exhibit that are ineffective?

2. What was a specific occasion in which you engaged in one of the types of bad listening? How did it affect the speaker or the conversation?

3. What specifically could you do to coach a bad listener to help him or her be more effective?

Content Module 10–9: Paraphrasing

One of the many listening strategies, paraphrasing is an effective technique that produces good results for many people. This module introduces the strategy and provides steps and tips for successful paraphrasing.

TIME

◆ 1 hour, 30 minutes

MATERIALS

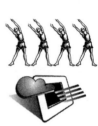

◆ Structured Experience 12–10: Paraphrasing Partners (chapter 12)

◆ PowerPoint presentation *Paraphrasing.ppt* (on the CD)

AGENDA

◆ Lead group through the first discussion question below. (5 minutes)

◆ Review PowerPoint presentation "Paraphrasing." (25 minutes)

◆ Facilitate Structured Experience 12–10: Paraphrasing Partners. (45 minutes)

◆ Discuss the key points. Lead the participants through the remaining discussion questions. (15 minutes)

KEY POINTS

◆ Paraphrasing is an effective listening technique to try to gain deeper understanding of a speaker's message.

◆ Paraphrasing can help to calm a speaker who is in an emotional state.

◆ Paraphrasing is most effective when you restate the speaker's words in your own words rather than simply parroting back to the speaker. This shows interest and care for the speaker.

◆ Paraphrasing may not be appropriate for some conversations, especially ones that are more quick and simple.

DISCUSSION QUESTIONS

1. Have you ever used paraphrasing as a listening technique, or have you had someone paraphrase your words back to you? If so, what was the experience like?

2. What is an example of a situation in which you could have used paraphrasing?

3. What immediate concerns do you have about using a technique like this?

4. What are some strategies that would help you use paraphrasing when listening?

Content Module 10–10: Empathic Listening

A primary type of listening, empathic listening is a common technique for diffusing emotionally charged situations or dealing with conflict. This module includes a formula to follow for empathic listening and the opportunity for participants to practice the technique.

TIME

- 1 hour, 30 minutes

MATERIALS

- Training Instrument 11–2: Empathic Listening Observation Checklist (chapter 11)

- Structured Experience 12–11: Empathic Listening Practice (chapter 12)

- PowerPoint presentation *Empathic Listening.ppt* (on the CD)

AGENDA

- Review PowerPoint Presentation "Empathic Listening." (25 minutes)

- Facilitate Structured Experience 12–11: Empathic Listening Practice. (50 minutes)

- Discuss the key points. Lead the participants through the discussion questions. (15 minutes)

KEY POINTS

- Listening empathically means to listen with the intent of understanding how the speaker feels, in addition to understanding his or her message.

- The goal of empathic listening is to enable the speaker to share his or her emotions without being judged or criticized.

- The formula for effective empathic listening involves acknowledging the speaker, reflecting his or her feelings, and describing the facts or situation as you hear it.

◆ The difference between empathic listening and paraphrasing has to do with emotions. The intent in empathic listening is primarily focused on the speaker's emotions, but the intent in paraphrasing may be to get additional information or clarify meaning regardless of emotion.

DISCUSSION QUESTIONS

1. How is empathic listening different from other listening strategies you use?

2. Have you heard of this technique before? If so, from what source? How did you react to it then? Why?

3. Think back to a situation in which you could have used empathic listening. What specifically would you do differently?

4. Why would some people hesitate to use empathic listening? What obstacles could get in the way? How could these be solved?

Content Module 10–11: Giving and Receiving Feedback

This module addresses principles and techniques for giving and receiving feedback effectively. An assessment is also included so learners can identify areas in which they may need to improve their behavior, because listening is a primary component in the feedback process.

TIME

◆ 2 hours

MATERIALS

◆ Assessment 11–7: Feedback Self-Assessment

◆ Handout 12–4: Feedback Role-Play Scenarios (chapter 12)

◆ Training Instrument 11–3: Feedback Observation Worksheet (chapter 11)

◆ Structured Experience 12–12: Fun With Feedback (chapter 12)

◆ PowerPoint presentation *Giving and Receiving Feedback.ppt* (on the CD)

AGENDA

◆ Lead group through the first two discussion questions below. (15 minutes)

◆ Administer Assessment 11–7: Feedback Self-Assessment. Ask for volunteers to share their insights about their results. (15 minutes)

◆ Review PowerPoint presentation "Giving and Receiving Feedback." (30 minutes)

◆ Facilitate Structured Experience 12–12: Fun With Feedback. (45 minutes)

◆ Discuss the key points. Lead the participants through the remaining discussion questions. (15 minutes)

KEY POINTS

* Giving and receiving feedback effectively is an important part of being a good listener. The feedback can be verbal or nonverbal, positive or constructive.

* The more specific and descriptive the feedback, the more helpful it will be to the receiver.

* It's important to ask the receiver if he or she is open to feedback at the time, as that can significantly affect the person's willingness to listen and be receptive. If the timing or location is poor, the feedback conversation may not go well.

* The person receiving feedback can focus on effective listening techniques to help him or her react well and concentrate on the speaker without becoming defensive.

DISCUSSION QUESTIONS

1. Was there a situation in which you received negative feedback? What behaviors did the person giving the feedback exhibit?

2. Think about a time when you received feedback well. How did this conversation differ from your negative experience?

3. How will you now approach your next feedback conversation, especially in light of your feedback assessment results?

4. What can you specifically do to coach someone in receiving feedback positively?

5. Why may giving feedback be uncomfortable at times?

◆

Assessments and Training Instruments

- ◆ Instructions for using assessments and instruments

- ◆ Assessments 11–1 through 11–7

- ◆ Training Instruments 11–1 through 11–4

Many worksheets and data-gathering instruments are available to the facilitator of an effective listening training program. This chapter includes assessments and training instruments that rate relevant traits, competencies, and practices, as well as other tools to assist in the learning process.

An assessment differs from a test because the responses to the questions in an assessment are not considered right or wrong. Most of the assessments are designed to increase self-awareness; this process helps participants focus on learning objectives to which they can willingly commit.

Please note that the major consideration regarding these training instruments is usefulness, not predictive power. They have not been tested for reliability or validity; they were designed primarily to generate data for action planning and personal commitment, as well as to promote learning about what is important.

Participants can use some of the training instruments during the actual learning process.

Assessments and Training Instruments

- ◆ **Assessment 11–1: Learning Needs-Assessment Sheet.** Use this assessment during an interview with stakeholders in the organization to help assess the needs of learners and of the client organization.

- ◆ **Assessment 11–2: Listening Self-Assessment.** This self-assessment helps participants understand and rate themselves on the competencies required to be a good listener. It also helps them focus on areas for improvement during training.

- ◆ **Assessment 11–3: Needs-Assessment Discussion Form.** This sheet helps participants gather their thoughts and provide information for the facilitator in a needs-assessment focus group session.

- ◆ **Assessment 11–4: Facilitator Competencies.** This form helps establish learning priorities for your own development as a workshop facilitator. It can be used as a self-assessment or as a follow-up questionnaire to solicit feedback from trainees after a session or at a later time.

- ◆ **Assessment 11–5: Listening Skills Follow-Up Assessment.** This survey is designed to learn how participants changed listening behaviors after attending training. It is best to wait three to six months after the training before conducting this type of assessment.

- ◆ **Assessment 11–6: Training Evaluation.** Use this form to conduct a Level 1 Smile Sheet evaluation. It allows training participants to provide reaction feedback for the workshop and the facilitator.

- ◆ **Assessment 11–7: Feedback Self-Assessment.** The results of this self-assessment will help participants review how adept they are at giving and receiving feedback during conversations.

- ◆ **Training Instrument 11–1: Memory Game Word Lists.** These lists are used during Structured Experience 12–5: Memorize This. One list contains words in a random order, and the other contains the same words in an organized pattern to illustrate that we tend to remember information more when it is clustered together.

- ◆ **Training Instrument 11–2: Empathic Listening Observation Checklist.** This worksheet is used in Structured Experience 12–11: Empathic Listening Practice. Participants playing the role of observer during the exercise should use this instrument to help them provide feedback to the speaker and listener in their group.

◆ **Training Instrument 11–3: Feedback Observation Worksheet.** This worksheet is used in Structured Experience 12–12: Fun With Feedback. Participants acting as an observer use this form to help them provide feedback to the others in their group who are playing different characters in the role-play exercise.

◆ **Training Instrument 11–4: Facilitation Preparation Checklist.** This tool is designed to help the facilitator prepare for a training session by ensuring that he or she has all of the materials and equipment necessary to conduct a workshop.

Assessment 11–1
Learning Needs-Assessment Sheet

Instructions: Use this form to take notes during interviews with stakeholders in the client organization to assess the needs of both learners and the organization itself. Be sure to understand the person's response to each question before moving on and writing a summary of what he or she says. Assure the interviewee that the responses will be both anonymous and confidential.

1. How do you define listening?

2. How would you assess your own listening skills?

3. In your role in the organization, how would listening skills training benefit you?

4. Would listening skills training benefit the organization at this time? Why or why not?

5. How would you assess the listening skills of others in the organization?

6. What specific behaviors regarding listening have you observed that should be addressed in a listening skills course?

7. What preferences do you have about how you might receive listening skills training?

8. Are others in the organization interested in receiving listening skills training?

9. Should all employees in the organization receive listening skills training, or should only select groups at a certain level receive training? Why?

10. How should listening skills training be marketed internally to draw attendees?

11. What results would you like to see for the organization after listening skills training?

12. What else can you tell me about your training needs at this time?

13. What other factors for success could affect listening skills training?

14. What questions do you have for me?

End the interview by thanking the person for his or her candid responses to your questions. Reassure the interviewee that his or her comments will not be quoted by name, just combined with others' responses to analyze common themes. Explain that the listening skills training will reflect the priorities of those interviewed.

Assessment 11–2
Listening Self-Assessment

Instructions: The purpose of this activity is to help you learn about what you need to be a good listener and create an action plan for self-improvement in your listening skills. Place a ✓ in one of the boxes to the right of each item, depending on how you see yourself today. No one will see your ratings unless you share them, so please be honest with yourself.

LISTENING BEHAVIOR	ALWAYS	FREQUENTLY	SOMETIMES	RARELY	NEVER
When another person is speaking to me, I…					
1. Focus on the speaker as much as possible.	☐	☐	☐	☐	☐
2. Concentrate on content of the message.	☐	☐	☐	☐	☐
3. Anticipate what the speaker is going to say.	☐	☐	☐	☐	☐
4. Establish eye contact with the speaker.	☐	☐	☐	☐	☐
5. Keep listening even if I disagree with the speaker.	☐	☐	☐	☐	☐
6. Nod, smile, or give other nonverbal cues.	☐	☐	☐	☐	☐
7. Plan my response in my head.	☐	☐	☐	☐	☐
8. Get distracted by environmental sounds.	☐	☐	☐	☐	☐
9. Take notes if necessary to help me remember.	☐	☐	☐	☐	☐
10. Listen without judging or critiquing.	☐	☐	☐	☐	☐
11. Interrupt the speaker before he or she is done.	☐	☐	☐	☐	☐
12. Think about issues unrelated to the topic.	☐	☐	☐	☐	☐
13. Pay attention to the speaker's nonverbal communication.	☐	☐	☐	☐	☐
14. Restate the speaker's message in my own words.	☐	☐	☐	☐	☐
15. Adapt my response to fit the situation.	☐	☐	☐	☐	☐
16. Can differentiate between fact and opinion.	☐	☐	☐	☐	☐
17. Look like I'm listening when I'm not.	☐	☐	☐	☐	☐
18. Ask questions to gain clarity about the message.	☐	☐	☐	☐	☐

continued on next page

Assessment 11–2, continued
Listening Self-Assessment

LISTENING BEHAVIOR	ALWAYS	FREQUENTLY	SOMETIMES	RARELY	NEVER
19. React emotionally to the speaker's message.	☐	☐	☐	☐	☐
20. Consider how the speaker may react to my response.	☐	☐	☐	☐	☐
21. Clarify meanings of the speaker's words if I'm unsure about their definitions.	☐	☐	☐	☐	☐
22. Allow speaker to vent his or her frustration.	☐	☐	☐	☐	☐
23. Think of different views on the topic.	☐	☐	☐	☐	☐
24. Display an open and caring posture.	☐	☐	☐	☐	☐
25. Create a nonthreatening environment.	☐	☐	☐	☐	☐

Analysis: If you responded "always," "frequently," or "sometimes" for items 3, 7, 8, 11, 12, 17, or 19, these may be areas in which you need to improve your listening skills, especially your focus on the speaker and how you filter information. You may also wish to address any of the remaining statements if you responded with "sometimes," "rarely," or "never," particularly for items 5, 6, 13, 14, 15, 20, and 23, which directly relate to providing feedback to the speaker effectively during a conversation.

Study this information and the following pages to see why those 25 behaviors are important to be a good listener. Then outline an action plan for self-improvement on the last page. Make sure it is a realistic plan to which you can fully commit yourself.

Why These Behaviors Are Important

The 25 behaviors that comprise this assessment are of particular importance if you would like to improve your listening skills. They represent areas you may need to address to become a more effective listener. Some of the behaviors, both negative and positive, warrant additional attention.

◆ **Concentrate on content of the message.** If you are concentrating more on the speaker's physical appearance, you may miss the speaker's message and meaning completely.

◆ **Anticipate what the speaker is going to say.** This is a common behavior among listeners and one that some may find difficult to correct. It may help to keep an open mind about what the speaker is saying and focus on the conversation.

continued on next page

Assessment 11–2, *continued*
Listening Self-Assessment

◆ **Establish eye contact with the speaker.** Good eye contact will signal to the speaker that you are ready to listen and will help you focus on the message. It also helps you read the emotions of the speaker to gauge your response.

◆ **Nod, smile, or give other nonverbal cues.** Positive nonverbal communication shows the speaker that you are paying attention and encourages him or her to continue to share information. This behavior will also help you remain focused.

◆ **Plan a response.** This is another behavior that many people engage in, whether they realize it or not. Since it may be difficult to correct, it's important to catch yourself if doing it so you can focus on the speaker and fully comprehend the meaning of the message.

◆ **Get distracted by environmental sounds.** When we allow external noise to interfere with our ability to listen, it will be harder to understand the speaker's message. It will also signal to the speaker that what he or she has to say isn't important to you.

◆ **Listen without judging or critiquing.** To be an effective listener, it is important that we take in a speaker's message without rushing to judgment or criticizing his or her views. Otherwise, the focus changes to you as the listener; this may harm your relationship with the speaker and interfere with understanding the message.

◆ **Interrupt the speaker before he or she is done.** Sometimes we are so concerned with our comments, opinions, or responses that we interrupt while the speaker is still talking. Make a conscious effort to stop doing this; it will greatly enhance your ability to listen and will help the speaker communicate his or her thoughts more effectively as well.

◆ **Think about issues unrelated to the topic.** Daydreaming or just thinking about other issues while someone is speaking can inhibit our listening ability, which can lead to misunderstanding or missing vital information.

◆ **Pay attention to the speaker's nonverbal communication.** Notice the speaker's facial expression, tone of voice, gestures, and posture to read his or her emotions more effectively and respond accordingly. If we ignore the speaker's body language, we risk alienating him or her with an inappropriate reply.

◆ **Restate the speaker's message in your own words.** While it may take some practice, this behavior effectively signals to the speaker that you understand the message; it also helps you gain clarity to provide an appropriate response.

◆ **Differentiate between fact and opinion.** This helps ensure that you are not allowing your response to be clouded by generalizations or false information, which in turn, may help the speaker view the situation with a new perspective.

◆ **React emotionally to the speaker's message.** A speaker may find this behavior offensive and may be unwilling to share information with the listener in the future. This may affect the relationship with the speaker and interfere with understanding the speaker's message or view.

continued on next page

Assessment 11–2, continued

Listening Self-Assessment

◆ **Allow the speaker to vent his or her frustrations.** In many situations, a speaker just wants to get some things off his or her chest; a good listener allows this to happen on occasion. It also shows empathy toward the speaker and a willingness to help. Keep in mind that it is usually beneficial to suggest problem-solving after a while rather than to continue to dwell on the negative.

◆ **Create a nonthreatening environment.** A relaxing environment encourages the speaker to share information, and it will also help the listener focus on the speaker and be more open to the message. This establishes a positive relationship with the speaker and leads to greater problem-solving.

Plan for Self-Improvement

1. Which two or three listening behaviors need the most improvement?

2. What steps can you take to improve these behaviors?

3. What are the first two or three steps you will take?

4. How will you measure your results and know you are improving your listening skills?

5. How will you personally benefit from improving your listening skills?

6. What support do you need from others that will help you to improve?

7. Who needs to know you are working to improve your listening skills?

8. How will you share this information with him or her?

9. Which behaviors are particularly important for your work life? Which are important for your home life?

10. By what time would you like to see noticeable improvement in your listening skills?

Assessment 11–3
Needs-Assessment Discussion Form

Instructions: Use this sheet to prepare your comments for the focus group discussion. Write the first thoughts that come to mind in response to each question. You may make any changes to your responses that you would like as the discussion progresses. Please do not write your name on this form. The facilitator will collect the form at the conclusion of the session.

1. How would you describe the listening skills of people in the organization?

2. What behaviors have you observed when others are listening to you?

3. What level(s) of employees do you think would benefit from listening skills training? Why?

4. How receptive would you be to receiving training to improve your own listening?

5. How receptive do you think others in the organization would be to receiving listening skills training?

6. What challenges or roadblocks may be present in the organization that could affect the success of a listening skills training session?

7. What would you personally like to see included in a listening skills training session?

8. How would you prefer that training be offered to you? (circle one)

   a. Private, individual instruction

   b. Half-day group session

   c. One-day group session

   d. Group session for one and a half days

   e. No preference

Thank you for your cooperation in this needs assessment.

Assessment 11–4
Facilitator Competencies

This assessment instrument will help you manage your own professional development and increase the effectiveness of your listening skills training sessions. Training facilitators can use this instrument in several ways:

◆ **Self-assessment.** Using the assessment to rate yourself on the five-point scale will generate an overall profile and help determine the competency areas that are in the greatest need of improvement.

◆ **End-of-course feedback.** Receiving honest feedback from the training participants can lessen the possibility of facilitators deceiving themselves regarding the 12 competencies. Trainees may not be able to rate the facilitator on all 12, so it may be necessary to ask the participants to rate only the ones on which they consider themselves qualified to provide accurate feedback.

◆ **Observer feedback.** Facilitators may observe each other's training sessions and provide highly useful information on the 12 competencies that are crucial to conducting effective listening skills training.

◆ **Repeat ratings.** This assessment can be used to track professional growth on the competencies needed to be an effective facilitator. The repeat measure may be obtained as often as needed to gauge progress on action plans for improvement.

The Competencies

Facilitators face many challenges anytime they lead a training session. The facilitator must be effective at many things to ensure that participants have their learning needs met and that the organization achieves its desired results for the training. This assessment contains a set of 12 important competencies that are required for effective listening skills training. Not all seasoned facilitators have expertise in all of these competencies, but they may represent learning and growth areas for almost any facilitator.

Here is a detailed explanation of the importance of each of the dozen crucial elements of facilitator competence:

◆ **Understanding adult learners:** Uses knowledge of the principles of adult learning in both designing and delivering training.

Effective facilitators are able to draw on the experiences of the learners in a training session; they must provide them with content and tools that they can immediately apply to fully engage them and help them see the value of the learning. It's also important to address the participants' various learning styles and give them opportunities to problem-solve and think critically so they can work through real business issues and develop additional skills.

continued on next page

Assessment 11–4, continued
Facilitator Competencies

- **Presentation skills:** Presents content clearly to achieve the desired outcomes of the training. Encourages learners to generate their own answers through effectively leading group discussions.

  Of all the competencies a facilitator uses during a training session, none may be more obvious than the need to have exceptional presentation skills. The facilitator's ability to present content effectively and in an entertaining way is one of the first things learners notice and is a large part of a successful workshop. Due to the nature of adult learning, it is equally important that the facilitator is also adept at initiating, drawing out, guiding, and summarizing information gleaned from large-group discussions during a training session. The facilitator's role is not to feed answers to learners as if they are empty vessels waiting to be filled. Rather, the facilitator's primary task is to generate learning on the part of the participants through their own process of discovery.

- **Communication skills:** Expresses self well, verbally and in writing. Understands nonverbal communication and listens effectively.

  Beyond presenting information and leading discussions, it is vital for a facilitator to be highly skilled in all aspects of communication. A facilitator should use language learners can understand; give clear directions for activities, involve trainees through appropriate humor, anecdotes, and examples; and build on the ideas of others; this will lead to training sessions that are engaging and highly valuable for the participants. Facilitators must also be able to listen well and attend to learners' nonverbal communication to create common meaning and mutual understanding.

- **Emotional intelligence:** Respects learners' viewpoints, knowledge, and experience. Recognizes and responds appropriately to others' feelings, attitudes, and concerns.

  Because there may be learners of many different backgrounds, experience levels, and opinions in the same training sessions, facilitators must be able to handle a variety of situations and conversations well; they must also be sensitive to others' emotions. This means paying close attention to the dynamics in the room, being flexible enough to make immediate changes to activities during training to meet the needs of learners, and creating an open and trusting learning environment. Attendees should feel comfortable expressing their opinions, asking questions, and participating in activities without fear of repercussion or disapproval. Monitoring learners' emotions during a training session also helps the facilitator gauge when it may be time to change gears if conflict arises, if discussion needs to be refocused on desired outcomes, or if there is a need to delve deeper into a topic to encourage further learning.

continued on next page

Assessment 11–4, continued
Facilitator Competencies

- **Training methods:** Varies instructional approaches to address different learning styles and hold learners' interest.

  All trainees have preferred learning styles, and one of the keys to effective training facilitation is to use a variety of methods to address them. Some people are more visual ("see it") learners, while others are more auditory ("hear it"), or kinesthetic ("do it") learners. An effective facilitator needs to be familiar with a variety of training methods in order to tap into each participant's style(s) and maintain interest during the training session. These methods may include activities such as small-group activities, individual exercises, case studies, role plays, simulations, and games.

- **Subject matter expertise:** Possesses deep knowledge of training content and applicable experience to draw upon.

  Facilitators must have solid background knowledge of the training topic at hand and be able to share related experience to help learners connect theory to real-world scenarios. Using anecdotes and other examples to illustrate how the training content relates to participants' circumstances and work enhances the learning experience and encourages learners to apply the information and use the tools they have been given. Facilitators must know their topics inside and out so they can answer trainees' questions and guide them toward problem-solving and skill development.

- **Questioning Skills:** Asks questions in a way that stimulates learners' understanding and curiosity. Encourages critical thinking.

  An effective questioning technique works well to assess learners' understanding of training content, as well as provides opportunities for them to analyze information and think critically. When learners ask questions, the facilitator is able to see where there may be confusion or a need to go over concepts again for better understanding. Similarly, when a facilitator asks thought-provoking questions in a way that invites participation, learners can brainstorm solutions to problems; they can also think through situations to help them apply the training content to the issues they deal with on a regular basis.

- **Eliciting behavior change:** Influences others effectively both individually and within groups. Gains support and commitment from others to achieve common goals and desired outcomes.

  This competency is important in two ways. First, facilitators must be able to persuade trainees to consider points of view that will lead to desired changes in behavior. Many times a facilitator is called upon to sell an organization's culture or policies, or to simply gain learners' participation to achieve the desired results of the training. To do this, a facilitator must be able to help trainees' understand and accept the organization's realities and practices while being sensitive to their own views. Second, an effective facilitator needs to know how to form small groups and work well with them in order to

continued on next page

Assessment 11–4, continued
Facilitator Competencies

influence groups to accomplish tasks, work through problems, and fulfill the needs of the group members. Drawing out the creative energy of groups through brainstorming or other activities and helping group members blend their unique knowledge and skills to achieve a common goal will lead to greater commitment on behalf of the learners to change their behavior for the better and apply the training content.

◆ **Feedback:** Gives and receives constructive, specific, and timely feedback and communicates observations clearly and accurately.

Providing learners with helpful feedback, whether formally through an assessment or informally through conversation, is a vital skill for facilitators. Specific examples that communicate a learner's strengths and weaknesses will help the trainee better comprehend the information and may also lead to increased self-reflection by the learner. Feedback can also serve as the basis for a coaching relationship for individual training and clarify the most important thing for the learner to focus on for his or her growth and development. The facilitator must also be familiar with a variety of tools to gather feedback from training participants to improve the learning experience; the feedback can also be for the facilitator's own self-reflection and growth.

◆ **Motivation:** Encourages learners to participate and achieve desired results. Generates enthusiasm and commitment from others.

One of the many responsibilities of a training facilitator is to inspire others to achieve the desired outcomes of a training session and to focus on their goals. While it is generally believed that motivation comes from within, a skilled facilitator can unleash the energy and enthusiasm of the learners by creating a vision that motivates and inspires. Providing meaningful learning activities and infusing fun into the training experience are just two ways this can be done. It's the facilitator's responsibility to channel trainees' motivation effectively into a commitment to achieving results.

◆ **Organizational skills:** Works in an orderly and logical way to accomplish tasks. Ensures that work is correct and complete. Presents ideas logically and sequentially for learners to understand.

The importance of this competency for facilitators is twofold. One aspect is that the facilitator must have good work habits and pay attention to detail. With any training event, there are myriad logistical and other details to take care of to ensure a successful experience. Work must be done thoroughly and accurately. A well-organized training facilitator typically creates well-organized, professional training. Another aspect of this competency is that facilitators must train in a manner that allows learners to absorb new content easily, as well as be able to retrieve it quickly. Information should be presented in a logical, sequential order for greater understanding. This also lends itself to a higher probability that the learners will use the content. The more organized the facilitator, the better.

continued on next page

Assessment 11–4, continued
Facilitator Competencies

◆ **Time management:** Plans and prioritizes time effectively. Balances important and urgent tasks and can work on multiple tasks simultaneously.

One of the many things facilitators do is conduct training sessions. They must also be highly effective at budgeting their time to tend to other priorities in their work, including preparing for the training, keeping accurate records, analyzing assessment data, designing new content or activities, and reporting to the client organization. The most competent facilitators are able to multitask and stay focused on the goals of the learners and client organization. Good time management is an essential part of helping a facilitator stay on top of all there is to do during any given day.

Facilitator Competencies

Instructions: If using this instrument as a self-assessment, place a ✓ in the box to the right of each of the 12 facilitator competencies that best describes your skill level. If using this form to provide feedback to a facilitator, place a ✓ in the box that best fits his or her level of competence in each area.

COMPETENCY	NO EXPERTISE	LITTLE EXPERTISE	SOME EXPERTISE	ADEQUATE EXPERTISE	EXPERT
Understanding adult learners: Uses knowledge of the principles of adult learning in both designing and delivering training.	☐	☐	☐	☐	☐
Presentation skills: Presents content clearly to achieve the desired outcomes of the training. Encourages learners to generate their own answers through effectively leading group discussions.	☐	☐	☐	☐	☐
Communication skills: Expresses self well, verbally and in writing. Understands nonverbal communication and listens effectively.	☐	☐	☐	☐	☐
Emotional intelligence: Respects learners' viewpoints, knowledge, and experience. Recognizes and responds appropriately to others' feelings, attitudes, and concerns.	☐	☐	☐	☐	☐

continued on next page

Assessment 11–4, continued

Facilitator Competencies

COMPETENCY	NO EXPERTISE	LITTLE EXPERTISE	SOME EXPERTISE	ADEQUATE EXPERTISE	EXPERT
Training methods: Varies instructional approaches to address different learning styles and hold learners' interest.	☐	☐	☐	☐	☐
Subject matter expertise: Possesses deep knowledge of training content and applicable experience to draw upon.	☐	☐	☐	☐	☐
Questioning skills: Asks questions in a way that stimulates learners' understanding and curiosity. Encourages critical thinking.	☐	☐	☐	☐	☐
Eliciting behavior change: Influences others effectively both individually and within groups. Gains support and commitment from others to achieve common goals and desired outcomes.	☐	☐	☐	☐	☐
Feedback: Gives and receives constructive, specific, and timely feedback and communicates observations clearly and accurately.	☐	☐	☐	☐	☐
Motivation: Encourages learners to participate and achieve desired results. Generates enthusiasm and commitment from others.	☐	☐	☐	☐	☐
Organizational skills: Works in an orderly and logical way to accomplish tasks. Ensures work is correct and complete. Presents ideas logically and sequentially for learners to understand.	☐	☐	☐	☐	☐
Time management: Plans and prioritizes time effectively. Balances important and urgent tasks and can work on multiple tasks simultaneously.	☐	☐	☐	☐	☐

Assessment 11–5

Listening Skills Follow-Up Assessment

Instructions: This form focuses on the outcomes of the training in which the learner recently participated. Please give your open and honest assessment of the person's current level of functioning. On the line to the left, write a number from 1 to 6 that best corresponds to the scale below to rate the person on some of the more important behaviors in being a good listener.

| **Participant Code:** |
| _____ |

1 = HIGHLY INEFFECTIVE   4 = SOMEWHAT EFFECTIVE

2 = INEFFECTIVE   5 = EFFECTIVE

3 = SOMEWHAT INEFFECIVE   6 = HIGHLY EFFECTIVE

The listener...

_____ Focuses on the speaker and eliminates or ignores distractions.

_____ Establishes eye contact with the speaker.

_____ Nods, smiles, or gives other nonverbal cues when listening.

_____ Listens without judging or critiquing the speaker.

_____ Avoids interrupting the speaker before he or she has finished talking.

_____ Restates the speaker's message in his or her own words.

_____ Responds appropriately to the speaker's message and emotions.

_____ Asks questions of the speaker to gain clarity about the message.

_____ Avoids reacting emotionally to the speaker's message.

_____ Allows the speaker to vent his or her frustrations.

_____ Displays an open and caring posture.

_____ Creates a nonthreatening environment.

Assessment 11–6

Training Evaluation

Your Name: _____ Date: _____

Workshop Title: _____

Facilitator: _____ Location: _____

Please circle the number that best corresponds to your ratings for today's training session.

ITEM	POOR	FAIR	GOOD	EXCELLENT
1. Quality of the workshop content	1	2	3	4
2. Applicability of content to my work	1	2	3	4
3. Quality of training materials/handouts	1	2	3	4
4. Quality of audio-visual materials	1	2	3	4
5. Facilitator's presentation skills	1	2	3	4
6. Facilitator's knowledge of subject	1	2	3	4
7. Amount of participant interaction	1	2	3	4
8. Time allotted for activities	1	2	3	4
9. Facility/location	1	2	3	4
10. Overall workshop rating	1	2	3	4

Would you recommend this session to a colleague? Why or why not? _____

_____

How will you begin to apply the training content after today's session? _____

_____

Assessment 11–7
Feedback Self-Assessment

Instructions: Use this assessment to determine areas for improvement for giving and receiving feedback. Place a ✓ in one of the boxes to the right of each item. Please complete the assessment based on how you tend to behave right now and give honest responses, as no one will see the results unless you choose to share them.

FEEDBACK BEHAVIORS	TO A GREAT EXTENT	FOR THE MOST PART	TO SOME EXTENT	NOT AT ALL
When giving feedback, I...				
1. Ask if receiver is open to feedback.	☐	☐	☐	☐
2. Give specific examples and observations.	☐	☐	☐	☐
3. Use a positive tone of voice.	☐	☐	☐	☐
4. Share the impact of the person's behavior.	☐	☐	☐	☐
5. Am aware of timing and location.	☐	☐	☐	☐
6. Keep an open mind to the receiver's views.	☐	☐	☐	☐
7. Practice good listening skills.	☐	☐	☐	☐
When receiving feedback, I...				
8. Am grateful for the giver's input.	☐	☐	☐	☐
9. Concentrate on what the giver is saying.	☐	☐	☐	☐
10. Keep my reactions and emotions in check.	☐	☐	☐	☐
11. Paraphrase the message to improve understanding	☐	☐	☐	☐
12. Ask clarifying questions if needed.	☐	☐	☐	☐
13. Listen more than I speak.	☐	☐	☐	☐
14. Avoid interrupting the giver.	☐	☐	☐	☐

continued on next page

Assessment 11–7, continued
Feedback Self-Assessment

Analysis: The results of this assessment can help direct your focus for areas of improvement as a giver and/or receiver of feedback. You may find that you score higher as a giver than as a receiver, or that you score higher on particular items in either category.

For giving feedback, if you rated yourself in the "To Some Extent" or "Not At All" areas for items 1, 3, 5, or 7, this means that you need to pay particular attention to the receiver's moods, emotions, and circumstances. If you scored low on items 2, 4, or 6, you may need to improve on the content of the feedback itself.

Under receiving feedback, ratings in the "To Some Extent" or "Not At All" areas for items 8–14 indicate a need to be more open to feedback and to improve your focus on the message and meaning of the giver. You may also need to pay attention your own reactions and find ways to minimize any negative or defensive behaviors.

Training Instrument 11–1

Memory Game Word Lists

LIST A (Optional: read aloud in monotone with little facial expression)

chair	boat
oil	soda
three	scissors
house	sky
ham	carpet
river	book
paper	travel
diet	desk
mice	blue
tree	cheese
store	rock
motor	cleaner
blind	agent

LIST B (Optional: read aloud with vocal variety and changes in facial expression)

ham	diet
cheese	soda
rock	three
paper	blind
scissors	mice
tree	desk
house	chair

continued on next page

Training Instrument 11–1, continued
Memory Game Word Lists

river	carpet
boat	cleaner
blue	motor
sky	oil
travel	book
agent	store

Training Instrument 11–2
Empathic Listening Observation Checklist

Instructions: This checklist is designed to help you provide feedback to the speaker and the listener during the empathic listening small-group exercise. Put a ✓ in one of the boxes to the right of each statement, depending on whether you observed the behavior as described. Space is included to share comments with the other participants.

DID THE LISTENER:	YES	NO	NOT SURE
1. Display an open and caring posture?	☐	☐	☐
2. Accurately reflect the speaker's feelings?	☐	☐	☐
3. Have good eye contact and body language?	☐	☐	☐
4. Show interest in the speaker?	☐	☐	☐
5. Avoid distracting behaviors?	☐	☐	☐

DID THE SPEAKER:	YES	NO	NOT SURE
1. Speak clearly so as to be heard?	☐	☐	☐
2. Correct the listener if necessary?	☐	☐	☐
3. Have good eye contact and body language?	☐	☐	☐
4. Listen when the other was speaking?	☐	☐	☐
5. Avoid distracting behaviors?	☐	☐	☐

COMMENTS FOR THE SPEAKER AND LISTENER:

Training Instrument 11–3

Feedback Observation Worksheet

Feedback for (characters' names): _____

Positive comments for the feedback giver:

Areas of improvement for the feedback giver:

Positive comments for the feedback receiver:

Areas of improvement for the feedback receiver:

Please share your comments with the others in your group.

Training Instrument 11–4
Facilitation Preparation Checklist

This instrument is designed to help you, as the facilitator, prepare for a training session by ensuring that you have all of the materials and equipment necessary to conduct a workshop. All pretraining activities and needed materials and tools are listed to help set you up for a successful session. Specific materials will vary based on the content modules you will be using for the training.

Pretraining Activities

☐ Reviewed learning needs-assessment data to ensure effective selection of content.

☐ Read and reviewed applicable content modules and structured experiences.

☐ Read and reviewed applicable assessments and participant handouts.

☐ Reviewed all PowerPoint slides thoroughly.

☐ Prepared additional anecdotes and examples.

☐ Practiced workshop flow and exercises.

Workshop Materials and Tools

☐ Content module and structured experience instructions

☐ Content module PowerPoint slide decks

☐ LCD projector with screen

☐ Computer and cables

☐ Power strip or extension cord

☐ Participant handouts, assessments, and instruments

☐ Attendance and registration sheet and/or participant sign-in sheet

☐ Participant name tags and/or table tent cards (if applicable)

☐ Facilitator and/or training evaluations

☐ Writing instruments (pens, pencils, and markers)

☐ Extra paper (if participants need it)

☐ Flipchart, easel, and markers (or whiteboard in training room)

☐ Masking tape to attach chart paper (if paper is not self-adhesive)

☐ Facilitator table or podium (to hold workshop materials)

continued on next page

Training Instrument 11–4, continued

Facilitation Preparation Checklist

☐ Watch or other timepiece for structured experiences and workshop flow

☐ Supplemental materials for structured experiences (such as articles and tennis balls)

☐ Toys or candy for participants at tables (optional)

☐ Facilitator's business cards (if external to the organization) to give to participants

◆

Structured Experiences

- ◆ Explanation of structured experiences
- ◆ Step-by-step instructions for using structured experiences
- ◆ Structured Experiences 12–1 through 12–12

This chapter contains 12 structured experiences to assist in the learning process. A structured experience is a step-by-step design that applies adult learning principles. Each experience includes:

- ◆ **Goals:** The learning outcomes that the experience is designed to achieve.

- ◆ **Materials:** A listing of all materials required to facilitate the experience.

- ◆ **Time:** Anticipated time allowances for each step of the experience. These can vary based on the facilitator and the participants.

- ◆ **Instructions:** Step-by-step instructions to facilitate the experience.

- ◆ **Debriefing:** Suggested debriefing topics and questions. These should be modified to meet the needs of the participants.

The Structured Experiences

Each of the following designs is self-contained. Although some of the experiences are designed specifically for learning outcomes associated with the module they support, others can be used in a variety of modules that the trainer either currently uses or is developing.

Structured Experience 12–1: Listening Buddies. In this structured experience, participants learn about and listen to each other in pairs. They share what they learn with the group to gauge their listening skills. It is part of Content Module 10–2: Listening Defined.

Structured Experience 12–2: What's That Sound? This exercise asks participants to tune in to the sounds they hear in the learning environment to help them focus on the world around them. It is used in Content Module 10–4: Types of Listening.

Structured Experience 12–3: Newsworthy Note-Taking. In this exercise, participants practice informational listening and their ability to recall what is said through the use of notes. It is part of Content Module 10–4: Types of Listening.

Structured Experience 12–4: Having a Ball. In this fun and engaging exercise, participants work in small groups to persuade each other to adopt a different point of view. It also lets participants practice listening without interrupting. This supports Content Module 10–5: The Listening Process.

Structured Experience 12–5: Memorize This. A well-known memory game, this exercise tests the ability of the participants to remember items in a list to check their recall for spoken information. It is used in Content Module 10–5: The Listening Process.

Structured Experience 12–6: Nonverbal Nonsense. This energizing and amusing exercise gets both the facilitator and the participants involved in communicating with the group only through nonverbal expressions. It is part of Content Module 10–6: Nonverbal Communication.

Structured Experience 12–7: Culture Shock. In this interactive exercise, participants work together to brainstorm the many ways nonverbal communication differs between cultures. It supports Content Module 10–6: Nonverbal Communication.

Structured Experience 12–8: Fact or Fiction? In this exercise, participants must decide whether information they hear is factual or inferred as part of a generalization. An intriguing interaction that typically gets the participants to think about their reactions, it is part of Content Module 10–7: Effective Listening Behavior.

Structured Experience 12–9: Driven to Distraction. This entertaining exercise allows participants to have fun by creating distractions while a speaker is presenting information to them. This is a powerful way to illustrate the effect of noise on listening and involve everyone in the group. It is used in Content Module 10–8: The Bad Listener.

Structured Experience 12–10: Paraphrasing Partners. In this structured experience, participants use the paraphrasing technique to respond to a speaker, switching roles so each has a chance to practice paraphrasing as a listener. It supports Content Module 10–9: Paraphrasing.

Structured Experience 12–11: Empathic Listening Practice. This common role-play exercise lets participants practice having a conversation that uses empathic listening skills. In groups of three, participants rotate being the speaker, listener, and observer so each has a chance to rehearse the technique and receive feedback. It is part of Content Module 10–10: Empathic Listening.

Structured Experience 12–12: Fun With Feedback. In this role-play exercise, participants take on various personas to have feedback conversations with each other; volunteers may also hone their skills in front of the group. It is used in Content Module 10–11: Giving and Receiving Feedback.

Structured Experience 12–1: Listening Buddies

GOALS

The goals of this experience are to

- ◆ Allow participants to interact and learn about each other
- ◆ Gauge their listening skills in a learning environment.

MATERIALS

None

TIME

- ◆ 5 minutes for introduction and setup of the exercise
- ◆ 15 minutes for discussion in pairs
- ◆ 10 minutes for debriefing

INSTRUCTIONS

1. Divide participants into pairs. If there is an uneven number of participants, form one group of three.

2. Tell participants to engage in a 10-minute conversation in which each partner shares information for five minutes. During each person's chance to speak, the listener may ask clarifying questions but otherwise should not talk. The listener should concentrate as much as possible on what the speaker is saying and should try to remember facts about the speaker. Time the exercise so participants know when to switch roles. In a group of three, the participants should divide the time accordingly so each has a chance to share information.

3. At the end of the 10-minute discussion time, allow the speaker and listener five minutes to share what each remembers about the other from the conversations. Provide a time update when two minutes remain.

DEBRIEFING

Ask for a handful of volunteer participants to share some of the more interesting facts they learned about their partners during the activity. Lead a discussion of how the group performed as listeners, as well as what it was like to listen in the learning environment with other pairs speaking around them. (10 minutes)

Structured Experience 12–2: What's That Sound?

GOALS

The goals of this experience are to

- Reinforce the idea that listeners can tune out background noise when needed

- Help participants focus their attention

- Get participants in touch with their hearing acuity.

MATERIALS

The materials needed for this structured experience are

- Writing instruments

- Blank paper for note-taking.

TIME

- 5 minutes for introduction and setup

- 10 minutes for listening to environmental sounds and sharing

- 10 minutes for debriefing

INSTRUCTIONS

1. Ask participants to take out a sheet of paper and something to write with.

2. Explain that for the next five minutes their task is to listen carefully to the environmental sounds that they hear and write them down (for example, noise from a car outside, the heating/cooling system, and someone coughing) without any interference from anyone speaking.

3. When ready to start timing, ask participants to refrain from saying anything for the duration of the exercise.

4. Once the five minutes have passed, tell participants to walk around the room and compare the sounds they noted with those of fellow participants to see if their lists match. Allow an additional five minutes for this.

DEBRIEFING

Lead a discussion by asking the group the questions below. The theme for the debriefing is to point out that as listeners we usually block out environmental sounds, keeping them in the background, yet it's impressive how much we notice when we focus. (10 minutes)

1. How many of you had lists that matched perfectly with others in the group?

2. For those who did not, were you surprised by this difference? Why or why not?

3. What are the implications of this exercise about how we listen and what we listen to?

4. What did you observe about yourself during the silent portion of the exercise?

Structured Experience 12–3: Newsworthy Note-Taking

GOALS

The goals of this experience are to

- Enable participants to hone their skills when listening for information

- Teach participants the importance of active listening

- Reinforce note-taking as an effective technique for memory recall.

MATERIALS

The materials needed for this structured experience are

- Writing instruments

- Blank paper for note-taking and writing

- A newspaper article of medium length (preferably one from the front page or local news section).

TIME

- 5 minutes for introduction and setup

- 5 minutes for reading a newspaper article aloud

- 15 minutes for pairs to compare notes and rewrite article

- 10 minutes for sharing rewritten articles

- 10 minutes for debriefing

INSTRUCTIONS

1. Ask participants to take out a sheet of paper and something to write with.

2. Explain that they will be practicing informational listening by taking notes as you read a newspaper article to them. They may use whatever style of note-taking they choose, as long as it helps them record facts from the article effectively.

3. Read the article aloud.

4. When finished, divide the group into pairs.

5. Allow approximately 15 minutes for the pairs to compare notes with each other and do a quick rewrite that captures the essence of the article based on both of their notes. This does not need to be lengthy; two or three paragraphs should be fine.

6. After 15 minutes, have each pair read their article rewrite to the group for approximately 10 minutes, then start the debriefing.

DEBRIEFING

Lead a discussion of how facts in the rewritten articles turned out to be similar or different from the original article. Ask participants to share how their notes matched those of their partner and what insights they have gained about listening after doing this exercise. (10 minutes)

Structured Experience 12–4: Having a Ball

GOALS

The goals of this structured experience are to

- ◆ Illustrate the difference between careful listening and listening with a goal of persuading others

- ◆ Explore the participants' behavior when attempting to influence others

- ◆ Build relationships among participants.

MATERIALS

The materials needed for this structured experience are

- ◆ Tennis or other small to medium-sized rubber balls for small groups of four to five participants (one ball per group).

TIME

- ◆ 10 minutes for forming of groups and setup

- ◆ 30 minutes for small-group discussions

- ◆ 20 minutes for debriefing

INSTRUCTIONS

1. Divide participants into groups of four or five people each. Have them move their chairs so they are facing each other in a circle (if possible).

2. Tell them to select a topic for discussion that affects all of them (if needed, use the suggested list of topics below) and take approximately 15 minutes to talk about this topic in their groups. Each person should try to dominate the discussion and convince the others to accept his or her view, rather than seek to understand one another. Remind them that the goal is not to get into a heated argument, but to have a persuasive conversation about the topic.

3. After 15 minutes, give each group a ball. Explain that they will continue their conversation for about another 15 minutes, only this

time, the ball is to be passed around from person to person until each has had a chance to express his or her opinion. Whoever has the ball "has the floor," meaning that the others in the group must listen to that person without interruption until he or she is finished and feels ready to pass the ball.

4. Once the next 15 minutes have passed, collect the balls and ask the participants to move back to their original seats.

LIST OF DISCUSSION TOPICS

Global warming	*Gun control*
Censorship	*Free trade*
Violence on television	*Universal health care*
Race relations	*Illegal immigration*

DEBRIEFING

When the participants have returned to their seats, debrief them on the differences between the first and second rounds of their small-group discussions. (20 minutes)

1. What did you observe about your behavior during the first round of conversation? What did you observe about the others' behavior?

2. How did it feel when others did not listen to your ideas? Point out how frequently this type of listening occurs in our lives.

3. How did behavior in your group change between the first and second rounds of conversation?

4. How did the exercise feel to you during the second round?

5. Explore how the one-speaker-at-a-time concept could improve the quality of conversations and the effectiveness of our listening in our lives.

Structured Experience 12–5: Memorize This

GOALS

The goals of this experience are to

- ◆ Allow participants to test their ability to recall information

- ◆ Demonstrate the effectiveness of grouping like items together as a memory aid

- ◆ Demonstrate the use of vocal variety and facial expression to assist with recall.

MATERIALS

The materials needed for this structured experience are

- ◆ Writing instruments

- ◆ Blank paper to list words

- ◆ One copy of Training Instrument 11–1: Memory Game Word Lists

- ◆ Flipchart or whiteboard with markers to record participants' scores.

TIME

- ◆ 5 minutes for setup

- ◆ 10 minutes to read word lists and exchange groups

- ◆ 10 minutes for debriefing

INSTRUCTIONS

1. Divide the participants into two groups, and ask one group to leave the room for a few minutes so they cannot hear what's going on inside.

2. Ask the remaining participants to take out a sheet of paper and something to write with.

3. Explain that you will read a list of words to them and when you say "go," they should write down as many of the words as they can remember. They should only start writing when you give the signal.

4. Read aloud the words from List #1 in Training Instrument 11–1. If you like, read this list with as much of a monotone voice as possible with little facial expression.

5. When it looks as though everyone has finished writing, have them cover their lists and leave the room, sending in the other group of participants.

6. Give them the same instructions as the first group, and read this group the words from List #2 in Training Instrument 11–1. If you'd like, use a lot of vocal variety and animated facial expression to test if that influences recall.

7. Ask the group out in the hallway to come back into the room.

8. Have all participants tally their scores of how many words they have written down.

9. Record the scores of the first group, and then record the scores from the second group. There should be a significant difference, with those who were read Word List #2 scoring much higher.

10. Give the first word list to someone to read to the group. Do the same with the second word list. Typically, some participants will start to laugh or comment once they begin to hear the groupings for Word List #2.

Note: Some of the pairs/item groupings for this exercise may not be culturally relevant or have the same meaning as they may in other groups. Feel free to create your own pairs/word lists that are more suited to the audience and culture of the participants if needed.

DEBRIEFING

Discuss the effectiveness of grouping common pairs or similar items to assist the participants with recall. If used, also ask the participants how vocal inflection, variety and facial expression may help with memory (be sure to explain what you did for the whole group if this tactic was used with group two). Ask the participants to name other situations in which they could use this technique, as well as to name some of the tricks or mnemonic devices that they've used in the past to help them remember information they've heard. (10 minutes)

Structured Experience 12–6: Nonverbal Nonsense

GOALS

The goals of this experience are to

- Demonstrate the power of nonverbal communication

- Build rapport among participants

- Have fun.

MATERIALS

The materials needed for this structured experience are

- Slips of paper (one per participant) cut from Handout 12–1: Emotion Word Slips.

TIME

- 10 minutes for setup and demonstration of acting out emotions nonverbally

- 20–30 minutes for participants to act out emotions for the group (depending upon group size)

- 5 minutes for debriefing

INSTRUCTIONS

1. Prior to the session, cut up slips of paper from Handout 12–1: Emotion Word Slips so there is a separate emotion slip for each participant in the training session.

2. Hand out one slip of paper to each participant.

3. Explain to the group that each person will come up to the front of the room individually and express the emotion on the slip of paper nonverbally. The rest of the group will guess what emotion they are acting out.

4. Choose three or four emotions from the list below (these are not included on the slips of paper) to demonstrate for the group.

5. When ready, ask for a volunteer to go first, and then work through the group until each participant has had a turn. Sometimes, if the group moves quickly, this can turn into a bit of a fire drill, but it is usually very fun and gets the group energized and laughing.

SAMPLE EMOTIONS TO DEMONSTRATE

Interest	*Growing Disinterest*
Boredom	*Contemplation*
Agreement	*Excitement*

DEBRIEFING

1. What observations do they have about the exercise?

2. What are the implications regarding nonverbal communication?

3. Explore how being aware of our nonverbal responses to others helps make us better listeners. (5 minutes)

Structured Experience 12–7: Culture Shock

GOALS

The goals of this experience are to

- ◆ Teach participants the differences in nonverbal communication that exist between cultures

- ◆ Demonstrate the power of nonverbal communication

- ◆ Build relationships among participants.

MATERIALS

The materials needed for this structured experience are

- ◆ Copies of Handout 12–2: Cultural Differences in Nonverbal Communication for all participants.

TIME

- ◆ 10 minutes for setup and forming of groups

- ◆ 15 minutes for small-group brainstorming

- ◆ 15 minutes for debriefing

INSTRUCTIONS

1. Divide participants into groups of four to five people each.

2. Tell the participants that they will have 15 minutes to brainstorm and discuss any differences they know to exist between cultures when it comes to nonverbal communication. For example, some cultures think direct eye contact is rude, and others do not. Ask the participants to draw on their experiences working with those with varied backgrounds and any traveling they may have done.

3. Tell the participants to select a representative from the group to share their results.

4. When time is up, begin the debriefing.

DEBRIEFING

1. Ask that a representative from each group share with the large group the cultural differences in nonverbal communication they discussed.

2. Distribute copies of Handout 12-2: Cultural Differences in Nonverbal Communication to everyone.

3. Read aloud some of the highlights of the handout, pointing out any differences the participants came up with in their groups. Let the participants know that they may keep this for future reference.

4. Ask the participants what this exercise illustrates regarding listening skills.

5. Ask if they were surprised by any of the differences. Reinforce the idea that the more we know about other cultures, the better our communication will be. (15 minutes)

Structured Experience 12–8: Fact or Fiction?

GOALS

The goals of this experience are to

- ♦ Illustrate how easy it is to jump to conclusions when listening to others

- ♦ Enable participants to gauge their own responses to generalized statements

- ♦ Share strategies for how to react to generalizations in the future.

MATERIALS

Materials needed for this structured experience are

- ♦ Copies of Handout 12–3: Argument Analysis for all participants.

TIME

- ♦ 5 minutes for setup and pairing of participants

- ♦ 20 minutes for analyzing statements in Handout 12–3 in pairs

- ♦ 20 minutes for debriefing

INSTRUCTIONS

1. Divide participants into pairs.

2. Distribute copies of Handout 12–3: Argument Analysis to everyone.

3. Have participants read through the inferences listed on Handout 12–3 and answer the three questions below each statement with their partners. Explain that they will have approximately 20 minutes to work through and discuss the statements and that you will then ask for volunteers to share their insights with the large group.

4. When ready, move on to the debriefing.

DEBRIEFING

Discuss the idea that we often jump to conclusions when we hear information. Talk about how it's important to stop and think about what is really being said and whether it is valid information. (20 minutes)

1. Discuss each of the statements on Handout 12–3 by asking for volunteer participants to share their responses to the questions for each item.

2. Lead a discussion of what can be done in listening situations to avoid making incorrect inferences. Talk about why it is sometimes difficult to distinguish fact from fiction.

Structured Experience 12–9: Driven to Distraction

GOALS

The goals of this experience are to

- Demonstrate the power of external noise when listening

- Explore solutions for dealing with distractions in conversation

- Have fun.

MATERIALS

None

TIME

- 10 minutes for setup and getting volunteers

- 20 minutes for presentations

- 10 minutes for debriefing

INSTRUCTIONS

1. Ask the participants for five volunteers who are willing to speak for two or three minutes about a topic that would help us get to know them better. Explain that this is a relaxed, impromptu presentation and they will not be evaluated on its effectiveness; it's simply for entertainment purposes and for the group to learn more about them.

2. Have the presenters step out of the room so they can collect their thoughts for a few minutes, and explain that you will call them back in one at a time to give their brief presentations about themselves.

3. While the volunteers are out of the room, tell the remaining participants to create some external distractions while the presenters are speaking to conduct an experiment on the effect of noise on listening. The goal is not be loud or obnoxious, but to engage in subtle behaviors that people may find distracting, such as tapping a pen on the table or coughing.

4. Select three to five participants from the large group to create distractions for the first speaker. Then, select three to five new participants to distract the second speaker and so on, until all the people in the large group have been assigned people to distract and each speaker has three to five assigned distracters.

5. Invite the first speaker back into the room and allow him or her to present for up to three minutes (give the speaker a one-minute warning when time is almost up).

6. When the first speaker is finished, ask him or her to take a seat and invite the next speaker back into the room, following the same procedure.

7. Once all of the speakers have presented, begin the debriefing.

DEBRIEFING

Explain to the presenters that the other members of the group were creating distractions as part of an experiment. Discuss how the presenters were or were not affected by the distractions and what can be done to handle distractions when trying to listen. (10 minutes)

1. Ask the speakers how they felt when trying to present with the distractions going on. Were they affected? If so, how?

2. Ask the other participants how the distractions affected their ability to listen to the speaker. How did they feel during the exercise?

3. Take a few minutes to brainstorm solutions with the participants for how to handle external noise if they are making a presentation, attempting to listen to a presentation, or are in conversation with someone. Note these ideas on the whiteboard or on a flipchart, if possible.

Structured Experience 12–10: Paraphrasing Partners

GOALS

The goals for this experience are to

◆ Provide participants with an opportunity to practice their paraphrasing skills

◆ Illustrate that it is possible to understand someone even if they disagree

◆ Demonstrate the power of active listening.

MATERIALS

None

TIME

◆ 10 minutes for setup and pairing of participants

◆ 15 minutes for paraphrasing conversations

◆ 20 minutes for debriefing

INSTRUCTIONS

1. Divide participants into pairs. If there is an uneven number of participants, form one group of three.

2. Tell the participants that they should choose a topic to discuss where they may have differing views or personal taste (such as current events, pop culture, or a moral issue).

3. Explain that the speaker (person A) should make a statement about the topic. The job of the listener (person B) is to listen carefully and paraphrase the idea by using such phrases as "It sounds like. . ." or "What I'm hearing you say is. . ." Emphasize that it is very important that person B only paraphrase to gain understanding of person A; he or she should not make any judgments about person A's statements or get into an argument with his or her partner. The goal is to seek to understand the other person's views. Person A should continue to make statements about the issue and be sure to correct person B

along the way if person B's paraphrasing is inaccurate. In a group of three, the participants should rotate roles so each has a chance to practice paraphrasing.

4. Time the exercise. After five minutes, person A should provide feedback to person B to indicate whether he or she paraphrased person A's statements well and whether person A felt understood. If not, person B may try again with some new rephrasing, or the pair may discuss what could have been done differently in the exercise.

5. Ask the participants to switch roles so person B now has the opportunity to be the speaker and person A has a chance to paraphrase.

6. After five minutes, allow person B to provide feedback to person A, as in step 4.

7. Once all participants have had a chance to practice and offer feedback on the experience to each other, ask them to return to their original seats.

DEBRIEFING

Ask participants the following questions: (20 minutes)

1. As a listener, how accurate was your understanding of the speaker's statements?

2. How did your understanding of the speaker's position change after using paraphrasing?

3. What, if anything, changed your view of the issue after listening to your partner?

4. What emotions did you feel by the end of the conversation? How did this compare to other conversations you have had regarding differences of opinion?

5. How might this process benefit you at work or at home?

Structured Experience 12–11: Empathic Listening Practice

GOALS

The goals for this experience are to

- ◆ Enable participants to gauge their ability to use empathic listening

- ◆ Demonstrate the effectiveness of using empathic listening

- ◆ Build relationships among participants.

MATERIALS

Materials needed for this structured experience are

- ◆ Writing instruments

- ◆ Copies of Training Instrument 11–2: Empathic Listening Observation Checklist for all participants.

TIME

- ◆ 10 minutes for setup and forming of small groups

- ◆ 20 minutes for empathic listening practice

- ◆ 20 minutes for debriefing

INSTRUCTIONS

1. Divide participants into groups of three people each. If necessary, the facilitator may join a group and participate in the exercise.

2. Hand out copies of the Training Instrument 11–2: Empathic Listening Observation Checklist to all participants.

3. Tell the participants that one person in the group will be the speaker, one will be the empathic listener, and the third will be the observer. Give them a moment to decide who will play each role. Whoever is observing should refer to the items in the checklist and be prepared to provide feedback to the listener after each round of the exercise (there will be three rounds total).

4. Explain that the speaker should share feelings about a work-related topic that has been a troubling issue for a while or something that is of concern to the speaker (either a real concern or one that the speaker creates for the exercise). The role of the listener is to use empathic listening as a response to what the speaker is saying. This should be a back-and-forth conversation with the observer taking notes. Remind the groups of the empathic listening formula and of helpful phrases to use, such as "That must be troubling. . ." or "As I understand it, you sound. . ."

5. Begin the exercise by allowing the speakers to share their feelings on a topic of choice for three minutes with their groups. You may want to provide the participants with a few extra minutes to think of their topics and write down some points that they would like to make.

6. When time is up, let the observers share feedback with the listeners for two minutes, and let the listeners share their reactions on how they did for two minutes.

7. Ask the groups to rotate roles so there is a new speaker, listener, and observer. Repeat the process in step 5. Follow the procedure in step 6 and move on to a third round so each participant has played each role.

8. When ready, ask participants to go back to their original seats and begin the debriefing.

DEBRIEFING

Discuss how using empathic listening will enable us to have better relationships, and how it is an effective tool in diffusing emotional situations. (20 minutes)

1. Ask for volunteers to share their experiences during the exercise with the large group: How did it go for them? How did it feel to them? What were some of their observations?

2. Discuss particular situations in which this skill may be helpful, as well as what the participants could do to use empathic listening more frequently in their interactions (that is, strategies for successful use). Emphasize that not every conversation may lend itself to empathic listening and that it gets more comfortable with practice.

Structured Experience 12–12: Fun With Feedback

GOALS

The goals for this experience are to

- ◆ Teach participants to give and receive feedback effectively

- ◆ Illustrate the importance of effective listening in the feedback process

- ◆ Have fun.

MATERIALS

Materials needed for this structured experience are

- ◆ Writing instruments

- ◆ Copies of Handout 12–4: Feedback Role-Play Scenarios for all participants

- ◆ Copies of Training Instrument 11-3: Feedback Observation Worksheet for all participants.

TIME

- ◆ 5 minutes for setup and forming of groups

- ◆ 25 minutes for small-group feedback conversations

- ◆ 10 minutes for volunteers to practice in front of large group (optional)

- ◆ 10 minutes for debriefing

INSTRUCTIONS

1. Divide participants into groups of three people each. If necessary, the facilitator may join a group and participate in the exercise.

2. Hand out copies of the Training Instrument 11–3: Feedback Observation Worksheet and Handout 12–4: Feedback Role-Play Scenarios to all participants.

3. Ask participants to review Handout 12–4 with you and explain that there are three different scenarios to work with. Walk them through the scenarios in the handout and format for the exercise. In their groups, they will have three rounds to switch off and play the different roles, working through each scenario one at a time with one person in the trio acting as the observer.

4. Give them a moment to decide who will be playing what roles to start for Scenario A. The observer should refer to the items on the Feedback Observation Worksheet and be prepared to provide feedback to the players after each round of the exercise.

5. Allow the participants about two minutes to review the scenario, and decide which roles they will play and what approach they will take for the first round. When ready, begin the exercise by asking the first two characters for Scenario A to start the feedback conversation. Emphasize that the players should remember to use the steps and tips they learned for giving and receiving feedback to carry out the role-play conversation.

6. Time the exercise. Give the participants approximately four minutes to have their first feedback conversations. When time is up, ask the observers to share their observations to the players for two to three minutes. Let the participants know that they have an additional two minutes to share comments with their groups, such as how they think they did during the conversation and what it felt like.

7. Ask the groups to move on to Scenario B and rotate characters/observers so there is a new observer for the second round. Repeat the process in step 5 above with Scenario B. Follow the procedure in step 6 and move on to a third round working with Scenario C so each participant has been an observer.

8. When ready, ask participants to go back to their original seats.

LARGE-GROUP PRACTICE (OPTIONAL)

1. Ask for two volunteers to do the role play again for the large group (a pair for each of the three scenarios, building on what they learned from their small-group experience). Explain that the first round will now be re-created and you need two people to role-play the first feedback conversation again (Scenario A), but only for two

to three minutes this time. Have the volunteers go to the front of the room and begin the role play.

2. After two to three minutes, ask the audience to share what they observed about the feedback conversation, and thank the volunteers for their willingness to participate in front of the group.

3. When ready, ask for two new volunteers to re-create the feedback conversation in round two (Scenario B) and follow the procedures in step two above. Do the same for round three feedback exchange (Scenario C) with two new volunteers.

Note: The above portion of this structured experience may not be suitable for all groups. The facilitator will need to gauge the personalities in the group and decide whether the large-group practice would be beneficial and enjoyable for the participants.

DEBRIEFING

Ask for a handful of volunteer participants to share their reactions to the exercise. Discuss how the participants performed as listeners and the role that listening played in the activity, how they used the steps and tips for giving and receiving feedback during the experience, and whether they found the steps and tips they learned to be helpful. (10 minutes)

Handout 12–1

Emotion Word Slips (Structured Experience 12–6: Nonverbal Nonsense)

HAPPY	DISPLEASED	IMPATIENT
APPREHENSIVE	DISBELIEVING	SURPRISED
WORRIED	THOUGHTFUL	SKEPTICAL
AMUSED	ANGRY	FEARFUL
SAD	ANXIOUS	DISAPPOINTED
DISGUSTED	CURIOUS	AWED
LOVING	HORRIFIED	FRANTIC
CONTENTED	EXHAUSTED	BASHFUL
FRUSTRATED	LAZY	FREE
EAGER	PROUD	UNSURE
RELIEVED	CONFUSED	ANNOYED
ALARMED	PAINED/INJURED	ASHAMED

Handout 12–2
Cultural Differences in Nonverbal Communication (Structured Experience 12–7: Culture Shock)

Cultural Differences in Common Nonverbal Communication

1. **Handshake.** Although generally adopted around the world, Southeast Asians press hands together; Japanese bow; while Middle Easterners and many Asians favor a gentle or loose grip.

2. **Direct Eye Contact.** Asians, Puerto Ricans, West Indians, some African Americans, and Native Americans consider it to be rude, disrespectful, or intimidating, or it may also be considered to have sexual overtones.

3. **Waving.** This means "no" to most Europeans. Europeans raise the arm and bob the hand up and down at the wrist.

4. **Beckoning.** Europeans and Asians raise the arm, palm facing down, and make a scratching motion with fingers. In Australia and in Indonesia, curling the index finger is used for beckoning animals.

5. ***V* for Victory or *Peace*.** In England, having the palm face inward toward the face is an obscene gesture.

6. **The *OK* Gesture.** In France, it means zero. In Japan, it means money or coins. In Brazil, Germany, and the former Soviet Union, it is an obscene gesture.

7. **Thumbs Up.** In Nigeria, this is a rude gesture. In Australia, if pumped up and down it is an obscene gesture. In Germany and Japan, it's the signal for *one*.

8. **Whistling.** Throughout Europe, whistling at public events is a signal of disapproval, even derision.

9. **Nodding and Shaking Head.** This has the opposite meaning (*no*) in Bulgaria, parts of Greece, Yugoslavia, Turkey, Iran, and Bengal.

Universal Hand Gestures

Meaning	Hand Gesture
I am tired.	Pressing the palms together and resting the head on the back of the hand while closing the eyes as if sleeping.
I am hungry.	Patting the stomach with the hands.
After eating, I am full.	Taking the hand and making a circular motion over the stomach.
I am cold, or it's cozy, or a sign of eager anticipation.	Rubbing the hands together.

Source: Axtell, Roger E. *Gestures: The Do's and Taboos of Body Language Around the World.* New York, NY: John Wiley & Sons, Inc., 1991.

Handout 12–3
Argument Analysis (Structured Experience 12–8: Fact or Fiction?)

Argument Analysis

Read through each statement below and answer the three questions that follow with a partner. Be prepared to share your insights with the large group.

1. The athletic boosters held a cake auction to raise money. We should have a cake auction too.

   A. Is there enough information to support the statement?

   B. Is the relationship between the statement and the support logical?

   C. What other information about this situation would be helpful to know?

2. If Dave hadn't laughed so loudly, I wouldn't have spilled my coffee.

   A. Is there enough information to support the statement?

   B. Is the relationship between the statement and the support logical?

   C. What other information about this situation would be helpful to know?

3. Jenny seems really organized, and she's good at doing work with a lot of detail to it. She'd be a great project manager.

   A. Is there enough information to support the statement?

   B. Is the relationship between the statement and the support logical?

   C. What other information about this situation would be helpful to know?

4. Bill was late to work again today. He's so irresponsible.

   A. Is there enough information to support the statement?

   B. Is the relationship between the statement and the support logical?

   C. What other information about this situation would be helpful to know?

5. All four of those candidates for the job are graduates of State University. They have such high-quality programs that I'm sure any of them would do well.

   A. Is there enough information to support the statement?

   B. Is the relationship between the statement and the support logical?

   C. What other information about this situation would be helpful to know?

6. Our profits were up last year by 7 percent and up by 5 percent the year before that. We should certainly have higher profits again this year.

   A. Is there enough information to support the statement?

   B. Is the relationship between the statement and the support logical?

   C. What other information about this situation would be helpful to know?

Handout 12–4

Feedback Role-Play Scenarios (Structured Experience 12–12: Fun With Feedback)

Scenario A (Round 1)

Amy, an experienced IT Specialist, was supposed to finish a project by noon for Kim, the IT Director. At 10:00 a.m., Amy told her IT Manager, John, that she would not be able to make her deadline. When John asked for an explanation, Amy said she has had to be out of the office a lot recently tending to her mother, who is ill, and she was relying on help from Steve, the new Network Administrator, who didn't get her some information she needed on time. Amy also shared that she worked three hours of overtime last night and came in early this morning, but she was still not able to complete the project on time. Amy also feels like she's lacking in some of the skills needed to get the work done.

Feedback Role Choices (Select one set of characters to play):

1. John provides feedback to Amy
2. Kim provides feedback to John
3. Amy provides feedback to Steve

Scenario B (Round 2)

Dave, a new customer service representative for a commercial airline, has been in violation of the organization's dress code policy since he started with the company one month ago. He shows up to work in tattered jeans and t-shirts, and appears generally unkempt. The policy clearly states that the dress code is business casual. When any of his co-workers make a comment to Dave about his clothing, Dave's response is typically to question why it matters since he just sits at his computer and is on the phone all day. One such co-worker, Pam, has tried to talk to Dave about it, but she doesn't want to push too hard, since he is of the opposite gender and she is not Dave's boss. Jack, Dave's supervisor, has heard other employees talk about Dave's appearance and question why he is getting away with dressing so poorly. Jack knows he should do something, but is hesitant, and there are other things to worry about. Julie, the Human Resources Director, has received a couple of complaints regarding Dave and is concerned about the policy being followed in the interest of fair play.

Feedback Role Choices (Select one set of characters to play):

1. Jack provides feedback to Dave
2. Julie provides feedback to Jack
3. Dave provides feedback to Pam

Scenario C (Round 3)

Kelly is a high-performing manager for an insurance firm. Lately, however, she has been dominating the discussion in team meetings and hardly lets anyone else in the group speak or express his or her opinion. This is intimidating to Scott, a new agent, and others

continued on next page

Handout 12–4: continued

Feedback Role-Play Scenarios (Structured Experience 12–12: Fun With Feedback)

in the group, and the situation does not allow for open conversation, exchange of ideas, or teamwork. People are hesitant to be critical of Kelly because of the strong relationships she has with clients and her high level of production and policy sales. Scott tried to talk to Carrie, Kelly's supervisor and team leader, about Kelly's behavior in meetings, but it was hard for him to think of what an appropriate approach would be and he dislikes going over people's heads. Earlier in the week, Kelly mentioned to Paul, another team member, that everyone seems to be clamming up lately in meetings and she seems to be the only one making a contribution. Scott seems especially quiet to her. Paul just stayed quiet, not wanting to disrupt things with the team.

Feedback Role Choices (Select one set of characters to play):

1. Paul provides feedback to Kelly
2. Scott provides feedback to Carrie
3. Kelly provides feedback to Scott

◆

Using the Compact Disc

Insert the CD and locate the file *How to Use This CD.*

Content of the CD

The compact disc that accompanies this workbook on listening skills training contains three types of files. All of the files can be used on a variety of computer platforms.

- ◆ **Adobe .pdf documents.** These include handouts, assessments, training instruments, and training tools.

- ◆ **Microsoft Word documents.** These text files can be edited to suit the specific circumstances of organizations and to fit the precise needs of trainers and trainees.

- ◆ **Microsoft PowerPoint presentations.** These presentations add interest and depth to many of the training activities included in the workbook.

- ◆ **Microsoft PowerPoint files of overhead transparency masters.** These files make it easy to print viewgraphs and handouts in black and white rather than using an office copier. They contain only text and line drawings; there are no images to print in grayscale.

Computer Requirements

To read or print the .pdf files on the CD, you must have Adobe Acrobat Reader software installed on your system. The program can be downloaded free from the Adobe website, www.adobe.com.

To use or adapt the contents of the PowerPoint presentation files on the CD, you must have Microsoft PowerPoint software installed on your system. If you just want to view the PowerPoint documents, you must have an appropriate viewer installed on your system. You can download various viewers free from Microsoft's website www.microsoft.com.

Printing From the CD

TEXT FILES

You can print the training materials using Adobe Acrobat Reader; just open the .pdf file and print as many copies as you need. The following documents can be printed directly from the CD:

- ◆ Assessment 11–1: Learning Needs-Assessment Sheet

- ◆ Assessment 11–2: Listening Self-Assessment

- ◆ Assessment 11–3: Needs-Assessment Discussion Form

- ◆ Assessment 11–4: Facilitator Competencies

- ◆ Assessment 11–5: Listening Skills Follow-Up Assessment

- ◆ Assessment 11–6: Training Evaluation

- ◆ Assessment 11–7: Feedback Self-Assessment

- ◆ Training Instrument 11–1: Memory Game Word Lists

- ◆ Training Instrument 11–2: Empathic Listening Observation Checklist

- ◆ Training Instrument 11–3: Feedback Observation Worksheet

- ◆ Training Instrument 11–4: Facilitation Preparation Checklist

- ◆ Handout 12–1: Emotion Word Slips

- ◆ Handout 12–2: Cultural Differences in Nonverbal Communication

- ◆ Handout 12–3: Argument Analysis

- ◆ Handout 12–4: Feedback Role-Play Scenarios

PowerPoint Slides

You can print the presentation slides directly from this CD using Microsoft PowerPoint; just open the .ppt files and print as many copies as you need. You can also make handouts of the presentations by printing 2, 4, or 6 slides per page. These slides will be in color, with design elements embedded. PowerPoint also permits you to print these in grayscale or black-and-white representations. Many trainers who use personal computers to project their presentations bring along viewgraphs just in case there are glitches in the system.

Adapting the PowerPoint Slides

You can modify or otherwise customize the slides by opening and editing them in the appropriate application. You must, however, retain the denotation of the original source of the material; it is illegal to pass it off as your own work. You may indicate that a document was adapted from this workbook, written and copyrighted by Lisa J. Downs, and published by ASTD. The files will open as "Read Only," so you will need to save them onto your hard drive under a different filename before you adapt them.

Showing the PowerPoint Presentations

On the CD, the following PowerPoint presentations are included:

- Listening Defined.ppt
- Types of Listening.ppt
- The Listening Process.ppt
- Nonverbal Communication.ppt
- Effective Listening Behavior.ppt
- The Bad Listener.ppt
- Paraphrasing.ppt
- Empathic Listening.ppt
- Giving and Receiving Feedback.ppt

Table A–1 Navigating Through a PowerPoint Presentation

KEY	POWERPOINT "SHOW" ACTION
Space bar *or* Enter *or* Mouse click	Advance through custom animations embedded in the presentation
Backspace	Back up to the last projected element of the presentation
Escape	Abort the presentation
B *or* b B *or* b *(repeat)*	Blank the screen to black Resume the presentation
W *or* w W *or* w *(repeat)*	Blank the screen to white Resume the presentation

Having the presentation in .ppt format means that it automatically shows full-screen when you double-click on its filename. You can also open Microsoft PowerPoint and launch it from there.

Use the space bar, the enter key, or mouse clicks to advance through a show. Press the backspace key to back up. Use the escape key to exit a presentation. If you want to blank the screen to black while the group discusses a point, press the *B* key. Pressing it again restores the show. If you want to blank the screen to a white background, do the same with the *W* key. Table A–1 summarizes these instructions.

We strongly recommend that trainers practice making presentations before using them in training situations. You should be confident that you can cogently expand on the points featured in the presentations and discuss the methods for working through them. If you want to engage your training participants fully (rather than worry about how to show the next slide), become familiar with this simple technology before you use it. A good practice is to insert notes into the "Speaker's Notes" feature of the PowerPoint program, print them out, and have them in front of you when you present the slides.

For Further Reading

◆

Adler, Ronald B., and Neil Towne. *Looking Out/Looking In* (7th edition). Fort Worth, Texas: Harcourt Brace Jovanovich Publishers, 1993.

Axtell, Roger E. *Gestures: The Do's and Taboos of Body Language Around the World.* New York: John Wiley & Sons, Inc., 1991.

Burley-Allen, Madelyn. *Listening: The Forgotten Skill* (2nd edition). New York: John Wiley & Sons, Inc., 1995.

Caputo, John S., Harry C. Hazel, and Colleen McMahon. *Interpersonal Communication: Competency Through Critical Thinking.* Needham Heights, Massachusetts: Allyn and Bacon, 1994.

Carliner, Saul. *Training Design Basics.* Alexandria, Virginia: American Society for Training & Development, 2003.

Covey, Stephen R. *The 7 Habits of Highly Effective People.* New York: Free Press, 2004.

Kemp, Jerrold E., Gary R. Morrison, and Steven M. Ross. *Designing Effective Instruction* (2nd edition). Upper Saddle River, New Jersey: Prentice-Hall, Inc., 1998.

Kirkpatrick, Donald L., and James D. Kirkpatrick. *Evaluating Training Programs: The Four Levels* (3rd edition). San Francisco: Berrett-Koehler Publishers, Inc., 2006.

Knowles, Malcolm S., Elwood F. Holton III, and Richard A. Swanson. *The Adult Learner* (5th edition). Houston: Gulf Publishing Co., 1998.

Kratz, Dennis M., and Abby Robinson Kratz. *Effective Listening Skills.* Boston: McGraw-Hill, 1995.

Nichols, Michael P. *The Lost Art of Listening: How Learning to Listen Can Improve Relationships.* New York: The Guilford Press, 1995.

Sullivan, James E. *The Good Listener.* Notre Dame, Indiana: Ave Maria Press, Inc., 2000.

Tobey, Deborah. *Needs Assessment Basics*. Alexandria, Virginia: American Society for Training & Development, 2005.

Verderber, Rudolph F., and Kathleen S. Verderber. *Inter-Act: Using Interpersonal Communications Skills* (6th edition). Belmont, California: Wadsworth Publishing Co., 1992.

Yelon, Stephen L. *Powerful Principles of Instruction*. White Plains, New York: Longman Publishers USA, 1996.

◆

Lisa J. Downs is the founder of DevelopmentWise, a consulting business in Redmond, Washington, which specializes in organizational development consulting and leadership, management, and personal effectiveness training. Downs was previously a Senior Learning and Organizational Development Specialist for The Growth Partnership, Inc., a consulting firm that specializes in the accounting industry, headquartered in St. Louis, Missouri. At The Growth Partnership, she worked as a workshop facilitator, a coach for the organization's partner development program, and as a curriculum designer with an  emphasis on supervisory and communications skills. Downs was also the Manager of Learning and Development for Clark Nuber PS, a "Best of the Best" accounting firm in the Seattle area, where she was responsible for overseeing the firm's training function and leading firm-wide learning initiatives. In addition, she established the Accounting Careers Program for the Washington Society of Certified Public Accountants.

Downs began her career by teaching language arts courses at the high school level. She earned her secondary education teaching credentials in 1996, which launched her career in learning and development, training, and curriculum design. Downs also spent time working for both commercial and public radio stations in the Quad-Cities area of Illinois and Iowa.

Downs received her Master of Science in Education degree with a concentration in Adult Education from Western Illinois University in 2000 and completed her undergraduate degree in Speech Communications in 1991 at Augustana College in Rock Island, Illinois. She currently serves on the Board of the American Society of Training and Development's Puget Sound Chapter and is an active member of national ASTD and the International Society for Performance Improvement. Continuing her passion for education and youth development, she also serves as a volunteer for the Washington chapter of DECA and Junior Achievement.